Dedication

In deep gratitude to my late parents

Venkateswara Rao Chintalapudi, Kusuma Chintalapudi, and Marudwathi Chintalapudi, my stepmother.

THE IGNORED MIRROR

— REFLECTIONS AS LIFE'S COMPASS —

WHAT TRULY DEFINES SUCCESS?
HARD WORK? TALENT?
OR SOMETHING DEEPER?

PAPARAO CHINTALAPUDI

ISBN
Paperback 979-8-89724-569-7
Hardcase 979-8-89929-744-1

CONTENTS

Acknowledgements... 9

Confidentiality & Disclaimer Notice 11

Foreword Dharma in My Sixties........................ 13

Prelude The Unexamined Life............................. 17

PART 1.0: THE INNER JOURNEY: DEEPER ECHOES 21

1.1: The Perpetual Dilemma................................... 23

1.2: Who Is Shaping My Self-image?......................... 25

1.3: Optics vs. Value: Deceptive Jobs and Titles............. 27

1.4: Emotional Baggage: Betaal on our Shoulders............. 29

1.5: Are We A Collage of Perceptions? 31

1.6: Expectations vs. Efforts: Who Charts Our Course?......... 33

1.7: The Freedom Dilemma: The Challenge of Letting Go 35

1.8: Rebirth: A Choice, Not a Promise!....................... 37

1.9: Surviving the Imperfect Careers 39

1.10: Work and Life: Opposites or a Flowing Whole? 41

1.11: The Art of Career Renewal: Shedding Roles................ 43

1.12: Obsolescence: A Shadow of Redundancy 45

1.13: Joy – A Self-Fulfilling Prophecy or Real? 47

1.14: The Unportable Success of Career Transitions.............. 49

1.15: The Fallacy of Desires 51

1.16: Life: A Journey Without Guarantees 53

1.17: The Gain Within the Pain................................ 55

Closing Note: The Inner Journey: Deeper Echoes 57

PART 2.0: KALEIDOSCOPIC SOCIETY: IN CONSTANT FLUX **59**

2.1: The Kaleidoscope of Contradictions 61

2.2: Societal Construct: The Maze of Expectations 63

2.3: Puppeteers and Perceived Truths 65

2.4: The Silent Chains of Approval 67

2.5: Wealth: The Idol and the Enabler 69

2.6: Faith: A Societal Push? 71

2.7: Religion in the Age of Science and Screens 73

2.8: The Fragile Individualism 75

2.9: The Silent Clash with Nature 77

2.10: Is Freedom a Fallacy? 79

2.11: The Burden of Too Many Choices 81

2.12: Not My Fault – The Blame Illusion 83

2.13: Timing: An Ignored Dimension 85

2.14: Results Are Elastic – The Power of Effort 87

2.15: Fear Trade – A Market of Anxiety 89

2.16: The Pandemic of Greed 91

2.17: Emotional Equity – The Soul of Societies 93

2.18: The Eternal Conflict: Seeking Peace Through War 95

Closing Note: Embracing Flux: The Rhythm of Progress **97**

PART 3.0: CORPORATE JUNGLE: LOST PATHS **99**

3.1: The Dilemma of the Many Faces of Culture 101

3.2: Alignment with the Boss: Imperative or Illusion 103

3.3: Incompetence Ascends, When Sycophancy Rules 105

3.4: The Ripple Effect: When Decisions Go Beyond the Boardroom 107

3.5: Duality of Corporate Decisions 109

3.6: Balancing the Scales: Ethics vs. Progress 111

3.7: Corporate Values: A Dichotomy of Optics and Actions 113

3.8: The Gold Fencing: Retention or Restriction? 115

3.9: The Corporate Catch-22 117

3.10: Dilemma of Stability vs. Diversification 119

3.11: The Misalignment of Scale and Vision 121

3.12: Silent Boardrooms 123

3.13: Merit – The Bottled Genie. 125

3.14: The Costs of Missing Ethos. 127

3.15: To Be or Not to Be: A Manager's Dilemma. 129

3.16: CXO Hiring – A Game of Hide-and-Seek. 131

Closing Note: Crucible that Melts and Transforms 133

PART 4.0: PHILANTHROPY: FINDING THE SOUL. 135

4.1: Corporate CSR Power: Outcomes or Optics?. 137

4.2: Purpose or Pretence: When Impact is an Illusion 140

4.3: Leadership Dynamics in the Social Sector 142

4.4: Inclusive Growth: Illusion or Reality? 144

4.5: Problems Eclipse the Passion 146

4.6: VUCA Challenge: The Social Sector's Acid Test 148

4.7: Donor Fatigue: The Silent Threat to Philanthropy. 150

4.8: Ignored Hierarchy of Needs 152

4.9: The Missing Element: Profit 154

4.10: The Path from Tokenism to Transformation 156

4.11: Dual Force for Transformative Social Good. 159

4.12: The Paradox of Giving as Receiving. 162

4.13: Collective Capitalism – A Philanthropic Path for Farm
Sector 164

4.14: A Framework to Make the Donor's Dollar Work Harder 168

4.15: Mindset Shift – The Success Imperative 172

Closing Note: Philanthropy: Purpose over Pomp. 175

PART 5.0: LEADERSHIP PRISM: REFRACT THE POWER. . . 177

5.1: Leaders: Born, Made, or Chosen?. 179

5.2: The Leadership Trinity – Purpose, Passion, and Profit. 181

5.3: The Courage of Vulnerability 183

5.4: The Art of Leadership Balance 185

5.5: No Exceptions: Even the Boss Needs a Boost. 187

5.6: Passive Leadership – Potential Curse?. 189

5.7: Transactional Leadership – Crisis Response or The New Normal? 191

5.8: Arrogance: A Byproduct of Success? 193

5.9: Alexanders: Products of a Competitive Society 195

5.10: The Leadership Mirror: When Crisis Reveals Character 197

5.11: The Price and Prize of Authentic Leadership 199

5.12: Empathy: The Emotional Glue of Leadership 201

5.13: The Power of Emotions in Leadership 203

5.14: Breaking the Ceiling – The Growth Mindset Imperative 205

5.15: Shaping Tomorrow – The Responsibility of Leadership 207

Closing Note: Leadership: A Rainbow of Influence **209**

PART 6.0: SUCCESS: ENIGMATIC AVATARS **211**

6.1: Vision to Velocity Is No Progress 213

6.2: Problems and Solutions: Yin and Yang 215

6.3: The Truth About Luck: Readiness 217

6.4: Success Without Integrity is Failure 219

6.5: Success Demands Intensive Pursuit 221

6.6: Size and Age: No Guarantors of Success 223

6.7: Suffocated Soul: Losing the Way to Success 225

6.8: Success Is Fragile: Handle with Care 227

6.9: Disrupt Success to Realign 229

6.10: When Success Templates Fail 231

6.11: The Courage to Not Know 233

6.12: Peace Through Conflict – A Mirage? 235

Closing Note: Define Your Avatar **237**

The Final Reflection. *239*

ACKNOWLEDGEMENTS

Countless people and events touch every life, each shaping our journey in profound and subtle ways. Significant moments may contribute little, while seemingly small encounters leave lasting impressions. Only through reflection can we truly recognise their impact.

I extend my deepest gratitude to all who have influenced my path—family, friends, colleagues, strangers, mentors, sages, saints, philosophers, books, organisations I have worked with, and even passersby. Whether knowingly or unknowingly, each has left behind invaluable insights that have guided and enriched my journey.

To my family, who believed in the impact of my work.

A special thanks to my publisher and editorial team for their professionalism in bringing this book to life.

And to my readers, who will engage with these reflections uniquely—I hope this book mirrors your journey, just as writing it has been for mine.

To all who have shaped my path—thank you.

CONFIDENTIALITY & DISCLAIMER NOTICE

This book contains **personal anecdotes, reflections, and references to organisations and individuals** based on the author's **experiences and perspectives**. It is intended for **educational, reflective, and informational purposes only** and does not constitute **professional advice**.

Mentions of **organisations, institutions, or individuals** are **purely illustrative** and do not imply **endorsement, criticism, or official representation**. All views expressed are solely those of the author and should not be interpreted as **factual statements** about any entity.

To uphold **privacy, integrity, and ethical responsibility**, the following applies:

- **Confidentiality:** Readers are expected to **respect the privacy** of personal stories and organisational references and avoid misrepresentation or unauthorised sharing.

- **No Liability:** The author and publisher assume **no responsibility** for this content's interpretations, actions, or consequences.

- **Accuracy Disclaimer:** The reflections are based on the author's experiences at the time of writing and may not reflect **current realities.**

By reading this book, you agree to engage with its content **ethically and responsibly**, honouring the **spirit of the personal and professional reflections** it contains.

FOREWORD
DHARMA IN MY SIXTIES

WHY AM I WRITING THIS BOOK?

This is a justifiable question for any reader to ask. I am not a celebrity with secrets to captivating the world or an audience eager to uncover the mysteries of fame. Instead, I am a humble career professional with decades of experience, a fair amount of career success, and an influence that has touched a few thousand lives. I share my journey not from a pedestal but as a fellow traveller on the path of life, just like you.

Over the past 40 years, I have worked in two contrasting worlds: forty years in the corporate sector and the rest in pro bono service within the social space. As a personal discipline, I return to global universities once every decade to recalibrate myself with a world that is always in flux. This unwavering commitment to learning, observation and reflection has shaped my perspective and purpose.

Inspired by the famous French philosopher Michel de Montaigne, who sought self-understanding in his tower study, I, too, am exploring wisdom—from the deep layers of my corporate and social space experiences.

Every life has a story, but few have the inclination, commitment, or courage to share it. I decided to be one of those few. Perhaps subliminally, I am inspired by the Hindu philosophy of Vanaprastha, a stage of life dedicated to reflection and sharing knowledge.

Through introspection, reflection, and self-confrontation, I have explored the lessons of my four-decade journey. This book invites you to do the same: dissect the paradoxes you encounter and challenge the fallacies you may unknowingly live with. The Ignored Mirror is a metaphor for our apathy towards self-reflection in the chaos of our paradoxically busy lives.

The ninety-plus reflections in this book will take you through my lens—into the inner chambers, intricate corridors of corporate jungles, struggles of social entrepreneurs, and tantrums of a kaleidoscopic society. They delve into the rainbows of multicoloured leadership and the labyrinth of societal constructs of success, offering perspectives to illuminate your thoughts.

Many of us turn to friends, family, or colleagues for guidance in moments of doubt or difficulty. We rarely seek solutions in books. Yet, personal experiences often resonate more deeply when explored through the written word. This book is not just a collection of reflections but a companion—a trusted friend or family member you turn to when navigating the paradoxes of life, leadership, and success. It is here to support you on your journey of self-reflection. Each reflection stands alone, like a bead in a rosary, allowing you to begin wherever your intuition leads.

Let me close with a reflection from the Greek philosopher Heraclitus: 'Nothing exists except atoms and space; everything else is opinion.'

The Ignored Mirror is my opinion—my belief that it can serve as a compass to guide your journey of self-discovery.

– Paparao Chintalapudi

PRELUDE
THE UNEXAMINED LIFE

"An unexamined life is not worth living."
- Socrates.

Socrates challenged his generation with this insight and continues to challenge every generation. The perpetual run of life rarely allows us the luxury of reflection, and without it, we risk affirming Socrates' timeless warning. Life is not only about successes or failures; it often resides in many neutral or grey areas with challenges and invaluable lessons. Unless we comprehend these lessons, we will miss the pearls of wisdom life offers to the diligent.

Paradoxes, in particular, can puzzle us and seldom reveal their true nature immediately. They present us with crossing paths that demand introspection. When we reflect on these moments, we unlock wisdom—not just for ourselves but also for those around us.

During one of my leadership programmes, a young participant from a tiny town asked me, "How can we learn from those who've gone before us—those who have conquered their careers and seen it all?"

It was a simple, humble, and profound question. It was not for career advice; it was a deep thirst for Lived experiences to shorten his learning curve. That question stayed with me for a long time and compelled me to write this book as a template for self-reflection.

Transformative Power of Questions

Over the years, probing problems with questions has become my *Swadharama* (an inherent nature) and has never disappointed me. With this modus operandi, I always find better solutions. This *Swadharama* has even earned me the nickname "mobile question Bank." I firmly believe that questions have transformative power and are easy to acquire, empowering us to find our own answers and solutions.

Let us begin with a primordial question many ask a million times in our adult lives and every sphere: "Am I successful?" This potent question creates an aura of illusion or delusion—irony.

The Illusions and Delusions

"Am I successful?"

The answer to it is rarely straightforward. Success is a complex concept with many avatars, interpretations, and dimensions. With its constructs and expectations, society often forces us to adopt its definition of success, making it a paradox of our lifetime.

As a teenager, I dreamt of becoming a medical doctor—a goal shaped more by external expectations than internal conviction. When I did not secure a merit-based seat,

I carried that "failure" like weight and guilt for years. Luckily, redemption came later when I was admitted to one of India's top business schools. Society around me coolly flipped the narrative. Once a failure became a celebrated success.

This experience left me questioning: How can the same person, with the same capabilities, be both a failure and a success, depending on whose yardstick? It seemed that I was only a character in the narrative, and it did not care about how I felt.

A Vedantin Question

While engrossed in this puzzle, I saw a striking observation from an Indian *Vedantin*: **"One will get first place because of the limitations of others."** He strips the absolute nature of success and says, "You are successful only compared to some XYZ." Simply said, many achievements—mine included—are shaped by circumstances, timing, and the efforts or lack thereof of others.

To clarify, if my competitor prioritised something else over our shared goal or lacked the resources I had, my success was not my own. It resulted from an interplay of many external factors and our efforts. This realisation compels us to ask ourselves honestly: What and Who has contributed to our success?

The Power of Asking

As I said earlier, questions have transformative power; therefore, I encourage everyone to gain the power of asking. This book helps you resurrect your power of asking. It invites you to peel back the layers of societal constructs, paradoxes, fallacies, and many more stereotypes and reflect on the hidden bare truths. This profound truth has the potential to drive our flourishing and fulfilment.

To reflect on this, let us turn to the stimulating question of the Chinese philosopher Zhuangzi, who posed a timeless question: **"Are we humans dreaming of butterflies, or are butterflies dreaming of humans?"**

Flipping the questions can challenge our assumptions and force us to ask: What is Real, and what merely pretends to be Real?

Perhaps Socrates was right—an unexamined life is not worth living. As we reflect, remember that the answers we seek only wait to be unlocked within another paradox. Begin your unlocking…..

Part 1.0

THE INNER JOURNEY: DEEPER ECHOES

Inner self: A vending machine of Emotions

The inner self is a complex, unpredictable entity. It acts, reacts, sulks, fumes, and, on rare occasions, stays silent. I think of it as the fulcrum of our persona and, intriguingly, a vending machine—one that dispenses emotions unasked. The challenge, however, is that this machine rarely operates under our control. We spend our lives striving to master it yet often fall short. Adding to the complexity, the outside world also seeks to press its buttons, triggering emotions in ways we do not always understand or consent to.

This inner self is the birthplace of our shared struggles, profound questions, and moments of doubt and triumph that shape our lives. Sometimes, we wonder: Is this inner self our ally or our emotional blackmailer?

Through the following reflections, we will traverse this intricate terrain together. We will examine how we perceive ourselves, confront self-imposed limitations, and unearth the fears we have left unexplored. This journey to self-discovery also equips us with a compass—to navigate life's complexities while remaining aligned with our values.

Our intentionality holds the key. When deep and clear, our intentions can transform these insights into a compass or an anchor when life's currents grow too strong. Ultimately, the power to chart this journey lies within us.

REFLECTION 1.1

THE PERPETUAL DILEMMA

"To be or not to be?" Hamlet's timeless question is not confined to Shakespeare's theatre—it echoes in our lives, especially when we face choices that test our values, approaches, and attitudes. How do we navigate such conflicts?

Throughout my career, I have often wrestled with the tension between honesty and diplomacy. I know many others share this struggle. While diplomacy has its place, it can sometimes dilute the purity of honesty, leaving us feeling like we have compromised something essential.

In corporate meetings, I have faced moments where I had to either:

1. Align with or endorse a boss's ideas—whether they made sense or not, or
2. Conform to Groupthink, which I find even more troubling.

Why do people fall into this pattern of ideological subservience? Is it fear of standing out, a lack of confidence in their ideas, or sheer indifference? Whatever the reason, the consequences are rarely positive. This tendency can damage not only individuals but entire organisations. For many, the motivation lies in external validation over internal truth.

I have often wondered whether Aristotle's Golden Mean could offer guidance in such situations. His philosophy suggests a middle ground between extremes—in this case, the starkness of absolute truth and the softened edges of diplomacy. The idea is to communicate honesty in a way that fits the practical realities of corporate life. But does taking this middle path mean ignoring our inner mirror?

Aspiring to live without such dilemmas is noble but requires an unwavering commitment to our values, which comes with its own costs.

So, we must ask ourselves: Are we ready to make those sacrifices, knowing they will bring challenges and uncertainties? If we choose that path, will we find the strength to face what it reveals about who we are?

REFLECTION 1.2

WHO IS SHAPING MY SELF-IMAGE?

Stoic Philosopher King Marcus Aurelius once said, "**It never ceases to amaze me: we all love ourselves more than other people but care more about their opinions than our own.**" His words struck a chord with me, as I have often reflected on how much power we give to others' views of us. How often do we let their opinions and judgements quietly shape how we see ourselves?

Every day, we encounter mirrors—not physical, but those formed by people's expectations, biases, and judgements. These mirrors rarely show us the truth. Instead, they distort our self-perception, often in ways we do not even realise. It is a little like Oscar Wilde's The Picture of Dorian Gray, where the portrait reflects something far removed from the actual person—except in our case, the distortion comes from the outside world rather than our own.

I learned this the hard way in my career. Let me share two anecdotes:

1. In one organisation, I was part of the "Golden Pot," a select group of high potential employees on the fast track. The company's belief in me became my mirror, reflecting promise and possibility. I trusted that image completely. But then, during promotion season, the role I was sure would be mine went to someone outside the "Golden Pot." There was no explanation, no feedback—just silence. That silence shattered the mirror I relied on, leaving me to question everything: Was I not good enough? Did I misunderstand the confidence my boss had in me? Or had

I simply overestimated myself? Disillusioned, I left the company soon after.

2. In another role, I worked for a boss who liked categorising or bracketing his employees. He placed me in the "Excellent" bucket, where I stayed for years. My performance reviews did not seem to matter, the label stuck. Then, one day, the bucket was not mine anymore. My boss needed to make room for someone else, and I was moved out. Once again, I grappled with a broken mirror, wondering if I had allowed someone else's perception to define my self-worth for too long.

Looking back, I have realised that the problem is not just the mirrors others hold up for us—how often we ignore our own. How much power do we give to these external reflections? How frequently do we let them overshadow what we know to be true about ourselves?

Corporate realities, like bell curve appraisals, may shape these mirrors, but they do not have to define us. The mirrors others create can be flawed. The only reflection that genuinely matters is the one we see when we look inward and ask ourselves about our worth and its alignment with our values and aspirations. Self-flourishing does not require too much external validation, I suppose!

How often do you pause to reflect on your self-worth independent of others' opinions, and how can you build a mirror that aligns with your values and aspirations?

REFLECTION 1.3

OPTICS VS. VALUE: DECEPTIVE JOBS AND TITLES

*"What is visible is not always real, and what is real is
not always visible,"*
– Lao Tzu.

His wisdom resonates deeply with the world of careers, where job titles often fail to reflect their true essence. Beneath the surface of impressive optics, I have often found a hollow core, while roles with less glamour can profoundly shape outcomes and identities.

Let me share an anecdote. I know the HR Head of a large conglomerate who has a unique approach to negotiating titles with new hires. He generously offers almost any title they desire—except the CMD (Chairman and Managing Director). Thankfully, he knows where to draw the line!

At one point in my career, I, too, faced a dilemma between optics and personal value. After spending two decades in prominent line roles with P&L responsibility across different verticals, I was advised to take on a staff position in the business transformation that operated on a larger canvas involving strategic planning and cross-functional collaboration. Still, I had less visibility in terms of public recognition. Although my reporting lines remained unchanged, the optics of the new role were starkly different.

Many of my colleagues strongly discouraged the move, warning that staff roles lacked the recognition and prestige of line positions. They were showing me their mirrors. On one hand, I had the comfort of a well-established role with status.

Conversely, I was uncertain about a less traditional and unfamiliar path. Despite these concerns, I chose the new role, driven by one key question: Would the lack of external recognition diminish my sense of achievement?

That was a transformative question. In hindsight, I realised that the role's optics did not define its value. The new position challenged me to think differently, challenge entrenched systems, and contribute meaningfully. While the recognition was quieter, the work itself was deeply fulfilling.

This dilemma between optics and value is not limited to individuals. Organisations struggle when leadership decisions favour short-term visibility over long-term impact. Flashy initiatives may steal the spotlight, but the quieter, foundational work ensures sustainability.

As Lao Tzu reminds us, perhaps the question is not about what we see but whether we are willing to look beyond appearances to uncover the unseen.

REFLECTION 1.4

EMOTIONAL BAGGAGE: *BETAAL* ON OUR SHOULDERS

"If you carry joy in your heart, you can heal anytime. But if you carry burdens, every step becomes heavier."
- Unknown source.

Indian readers may recall the timeless tales of Vikram and *Betaal*, written by Somdev Bhatt in the 11th century. *Betaal*, a ghost or vampire, clung to King Vikramaditya's shoulders, whispering riddles and questions that tested his resolve and wisdom. Emotional baggage, like *Betaal*, clings to our memories, quietly influencing our choices and shaping how we see ourselves and the world.

Failures, more than successes, linger in our minds with uncanny persistence. My inability to gain admission to medical school stayed with me far too long, often casting shadows of doubt over my worth. Even as I reached professional milestones, that *Betaal* of failure reframed my achievements as acts of redemption rather than genuine progress. I often ask myself: Am I truly moving forward or simply trying to escape the weight of my past failures?

This presence is not just persistent; it can also be overwhelming. A minor setback today can feel disproportionately painful because it stirs echoes of old wounds. Past compliments and validation often fail to penetrate or heal these wounds.

Through deep self-confrontation, I have realised that if we confront these echoes—refusing to let them dictate our present—the *Betaal* begins to lose its grip, becoming quieter and its weight diminished. This is not a single moment of realisation—it is an ongoing practice of self-confrontation, reflection, and frequent visits to my Ignored Mirror. Living in the present can gradually narrow the power the past holds over us. The past can shape us, but it does not have to define or destroy our future.

Of course, like in the Vikram-*Betaal* stories, the *Betaal* occasionally whispers wisdom, too. Just as *Betaal's* riddles ultimately made King Vikramaditya wiser, our past failures can whisper important truths if we listen carefully. These whispers of wisdom from our past struggles can be a compass with hard-earned insight.

The question is not whether we carry *Betaals* but whether we are willing to put them down before they take over our lives. Can we confront the echoes of our past, transforming their whispers into wisdom that guides our future?

REFLECTION 1.5

ARE WE A COLLAGE OF PERCEPTIONS?

"We do not see things as they are; we see them as we are."
– Anaïs Nin.

American-French writer Anaïs Nin aptly observed that our perceptions, beliefs, and experiences act as a lens through which we interpret the world. Similarly, the world interprets us in countless ways, shaped by selective perceptions and inevitable distortions.

Have you ever felt trapped by how others perceive you? It is like being caught in a hall of mirrors, where each reflection shows a version of you filtered through someone else's view. These fragmented perceptions—formed in fleeting interactions or moments—often start to build an image of us. We adopt these fragments without realising them, allowing them to shape our identity and sometimes become self-fulfilling prophecies.

I once tested this idea on myself during a class discussion at the University of Notre Dame. I asked my cohort to share their perceptions of me. Their answers ranged from "inquisitive" and "intentional" to "sarcastic" and "affectionate." Each response revealed a facet of me, but none painted the complete picture. This exercise taught me a powerful lesson: while others' views can offer insights, they are often incomplete and, at times, misleading. It was a stark reminder of how perceptions influence our sense of self.

No matter how elaborate, a collage of perceptions can never fully capture the complexity of who we are. Yet, we often adjust our behaviour to fit these labels, even when they do not align with our true selves. Over time, this alignment creates an invisible construct—a perceptual prison built by the world around us and reinforced by our acceptance of it. We become its inmates, often without realising we hold the key to freedom.

If I extend this reflection to my pet Pomeranian, Rushi, and ask him who I am, his answer would be refreshingly simple: "a two-legged friendly creature that makes strange noises." My identity, achievements, and carefully curated self-image mean nothing to him.

Rushi's perception of me as a friendly, noise-making creature is not wrong—it is simply one fragment, one perspective among many. This serves as a reminder to question the universality of self-perceptions and others' opinions. Our definitions of ourselves and the world are interpretations, not absolute truths. Recognising this helps us break down the walls of our perceptual prison and make room for a more authentic understanding of who we are. Apart from finding our authentic selves under these layers of perception, we must live with these ever-evolving identities, which are even intertwined with our various roles.

Are we willing to see beyond the fragments others project and the ones we have accepted? Or will we let these pieces define a never-complete whole?

REFLECTION 1.6

EXPECTATIONS VS. EFFORTS:
WHO CHARTS OUR COURSE?

"Desire alone does not light a lamp; effort is the oil that fuels it."
- Anonymous.

Does this not challenge Paulo Coelho's popular notion: "When you want something, all the universe conspires to help you achieve it"? While Coelho's words inspire us to dream, they can also mislead us into believing that desire alone guarantees success. The truth is far less poetic: the Universe owes us no favours. Success is not handed to us; it is earned through consistent and deliberate effort, putting us in the driver's seat of our destiny.

Consider the analogy of material balancing chemistry equations: the inputs always determine the output. For instance, if we want a flourishing career or meaningful relationships, our investment must match our desired outcomes. The effort is the key determinant in this equation, while luck and prayers serve as occasional sparks—unreliable and unpredictable catalysts. Stretching expectations without aligning them with deliberate action often leads to frustration and disappointment.

I recall a story about a friend who once visited an astrologer. The astrologer confidently predicted that my friend would become a famous auditor, citing his current apprenticeship as proof of this certainty. Convinced that success was preordained, my friend relaxed his efforts, believing the outcome was inevitable. Predictably, he never achieved the fame he had been promised. His reliance on expectations, without action, became his downfall.

Expectations can inspire us to dream big, aim high, and push further. But unchecked, they risk becoming burdens, creating unrealistic demands, and draining our peace of mind. Striking a balance between aspirations and reality is essential to shaping a meaningful and fulfilling life.

Managing expectations is not about lowering them but aligning them with deliberate effort and personal values. When we do this, expectations transform from heavy burdens into empowering tools for growth, guiding us toward authentic success.

Desires may set the goal, but only effort fuels the journey. Are your dreams lighting the path forward, or are they waiting for the oil of effort to bring them to life?

REFLECTION 1.7

THE FREEDOM DILEMMA: THE CHALLENGE OF LETTING GO

"In the process of letting go, you will lose many things from the past, but you will find yourself."
– Deepak Chopra.

Freedom and letting go might seem like synonyms, but in reality, they drive each other in unexpected ways. We all crave freedom—liberation from societal norms, rigid roles, or limiting beliefs. Yet, achieving it does not always bring the relief we expect. Often, freedom expands choices but also increases responsibilities. It opens vast possibilities but offers no clear direction. This is the paradox of freedom: it liberates us and challenges us to use it wisely.

Nature offers profound lessons in letting go. Over millennia, rivers have carved new courses, mountains have eroded into valleys, and forests have regenerated. Even our bodies follow this principle of renewal—scientists remind us that parts of us are born and die daily. A six-pound newborn grows into a 200-pound adult through continuous cycles of growth and decay. Letting go is fundamental to survival and essential for balance, transformation, and evolution.

Yet, as humans, we resist. While we may accept the physical changes in our bodies, we cling stubbornly to our egos, beliefs, possessions, and roles—things that often no longer serve us. Why do we hold on so tightly to what we cannot keep? Do we mistake letting go for failure rather than seeing it as an opportunity for renewal?

Breaking free from rigid roles in my career brought immense relief—an invigorating sense of liberation. But it also left me grappling with the challenge of what to do with my newfound freedom. Without a clear purpose or structure, liberation can feel hollow. I have observed the same in organisations: attempts to flatten hierarchies often promote innovation but leave teams directionless without leadership. Freedom without self-control or purpose can spiral into chaos.

Self-control and freedom may appear as opposites, but they complement each other. Without self-control, freedom risks becoming disorder, and self-control becomes oppressive. The balance lies in understanding what to hold on to and what to let go of—a delicate act of discernment that mirrors nature's wisdom.

Letting go is not a loss but an act of trust in ourselves and the renewal process. Despite knowing that life will eventually require us to let go, we cling to our egos, possessions, and roles. Why do we resist what is natural?

Isn't freedom about choosing what truly matters, not the absence of constraints? Similarly, is not letting go an act of courage to create space for transformation, not surrendering as we fear?

What are you holding on to that no longer serves you, and how might letting open the door to a freer, fuller life?

REFLECTION 1.8

REBIRTH: A CHOICE, NOT A PROMISE!

"Each morning, we are born again. What we do today is what matters most."
– Buddha.

On a lighter note, rebirth in some religious contexts feels like the elusive rewards promised in a corporate bonus system—offered for the future, contingent on performance today, but often beyond reach. Like variable pay, the promise of rebirth often feels distant and unattainable, yet it has been sold to millions over centuries to encourage moral and righteous living.

Religious texts frequently use the concept of rebirth to inspire people to walk the righteous path. While the metaphor is powerful, its literal interpretation can leave us questioning its plausibility. Spiritual philosophers, however, have often viewed rebirth not as a distant promise but as a call to reset and renew in this life whenever we stray from our path.

Buddha's story is itself a testament to rebirth. Born into royalty, Prince Siddhartha renounced his princely comforts to seek enlightenment, ultimately becoming Gautama Buddha. His transformation was not tied to another life but was a deliberate, profound shift within this one. Siddhartha's story reminds us that rebirth is not bound by time—it is a conscious realignment with purpose, available at any moment.

Once a shy lawyer, Mahatma Gandhi redefined himself as a global icon of nonviolent resistance. Nelson Mandela emerged from 27 years of imprisonment with a renewed purpose: to unite a divided nation. These examples remind us that rebirth does not demand a new life; it calls for courage, awareness, and the willingness to let go of what no longer serves us.

Rebirth does not carry the weight of past lives or karmic debts. Instead, it is a clean slate—a chance to free ourselves from yesterday's mistakes, regrets, or expectations. Life always provides opportunities to reset. Rebirth does not come from passively waiting for change but actively cultivating self-awareness and a deep craving for fulfilment.

Letting go is central to this process. Releasing past burdens—whether emotional, societal, or self-imposed—creates space for transformation. Siddhartha let go of his royal identity, Gandhi released his insecurities, and Mandela chose forgiveness over anger. In each case, rebirth was a conscious act of renewal.

Rebirth does not require dramatic life changes. Sometimes, it is as simple as starting your day with fresh resolve or forgiving yourself for a mistake. Can we not pause momentarily and reflect, "What is one small step I can take today to move closer to the person I want to become?"

Imagine a friend asking, "If you could start fresh right now, what's one thing you would leave behind?" How would you respond? Would it be fear, regret, or a long-held expectation? And then, ask ourselves, "What is stopping us from letting go and stepping into a new beginning today?"

Rebirth is an invitation—a chance to realign with what truly matters, here and now. So, what will it take for you to embrace your moment of renewal?

REFLECTION 1.9

SURVIVING THE IMPERFECT CAREERS

"Life is not about waiting for the storm to pass, but learning to dance in the rain."
– Anonymous.

Much like water, careers Flow along the paths of least resistance, settling into the best available alternatives at any moment. The decisions we make at each stage of life are often the best we can manage under the circumstances. And yet, we sometimes indulge in wishful thoughts of "what could have been." But let's be honest—those fantasies are just that: fantasies. For most of us, this principle holds, even as a fortunate few stumble into perfect opportunities by sheer coincidence.

Pursuing a "perfect career"—a flawless job or ideal promotion—is a common yet draining illusion. How many years are spent chasing this mirage, waiting for something better while overlooking the opportunities already at hand? Rarely do solutions to career dilemmas arrive in neatly wrapped packages. Instead, they come in fragments, leaving us responsible for piecing them together into something meaningful.

Waiting for perfection often conceals deeper issues: fear of failure, inertia, or procrastination. It is a never-ending cycle of worry—about not progressing fast enough or missing the next big opportunity. But this cycle is unnecessary. Progress does not need to be perfect; it needs to move forward. Concentrating on the opportunities before us can redirect our energy from chasing illusions to constructing something tangible and fulfilling.

As we navigate the realities of imperfect careers, a question often arises: "Can I find fulfilment in what I'm doing right now, or am I always waiting for something better?" It is worth asking yourself: What if your path isn't a mistake but an opportunity to create meaning? Is not it possible that the fragments of your work—no matter how scattered—can be pieced together into something genuinely gratifying?

Often, colleagues would ask me, "Do you think I can find the perfect job?" My standard reply was, "Probably not. But you can find your Flow—that state where you're so immersed in what you're doing that time fades away, and the work itself feels fulfilling. Is not that the closest thing to perfection we can achieve?"

So, here is a thought: What small step can you take today to stop chasing illusions and step into the Flow, where fulfilment becomes the natural outcome?

REFLECTION 1.10

WORK AND LIFE: OPPOSITES OR A FLOWING WHOLE?

"Flow is the process of total involvement with life."
– Mihaly Csiksgentmihalyi.

We have discussed how Flow—being fully immersed in the present—can help us manage imperfections. Mihaly Csikszentmihalyi, an American Psychologist, described Flow as a state of complete absorption in an activity, offering a psychological concept and a perspective on finding fulfilment in work and life. Flow is not about achieving perfection; it is about engaging so deeply in what we do that time and worries disappear.

In my mid-forties, the term "work-life balance" became a buzzword. I found it amusing and puzzling. If someone seeks balance, doesn't it imply they are dissatisfied with one of the two—mostly work? My counter would often be, "If your work energises rather than drains you, balance is not about separation—it is about integration. Is not that more rewarding?"

Flow moments are transformative. Whether you're solving a challenging problem, creating something meaningful, playing a sport, or immersing yourself in a deep conversation, these are the times when life feels aligned. Such moments do not just feel good; they connect us to our purpose and inspire us to move forward.

But not every task brings Flow. Some are mundane or repetitive. This is where the concept of balance often comes in—not as a division of time but as a way to realign. Work-life balance is less about separating the two and more about recognising when we are out of alignment and using Flow to regain that harmony.

When someone asks, "Does this mean we should ignore mundane tasks?" the answer is clear: "No. It is about creating space for what fulfils us amidst the ordinary. It is about weaving moments of Flow into our routine, not letting the mundane define it."

Work-life balance is often a response to unmet expectations. It arises when we fail to find Flow in our work or personal lives, leaving us seeking balance to fill those voids. But what if we focus on cultivating Flow instead of dividing our time? What if we stopped seeing work and life as opposites and instead embraced their integration?

Flow is not about endless productivity; it is about presence and purpose. It can transform fragmented attention into a timeless, fulfilling experience, blending work and life into a harmonious whole.

What if the key isn't balancing work and life but flowing through both? How will you create moments of immersion today?

REFLECTION 1.11

THE ART OF CAREER RENEWAL: SHEDDING ROLES

"The snake which cannot cast its skin must die."
– Friedrich Nietzsche, German Philosopher.

Like life, careers have natural rhythms—a climb of energy and achievement followed by an inevitable descent. While unsettling, this latter phase is integral to our professional journey. It often provokes worries like, "Who am I without this role?" or "What's my worth beyond work?" Nietzsche's metaphor of the snake offers a crucial insight: shedding what no longer serves us is not just necessary—it is essential for survival.

Descent does not mean decline—it signals a transition. Unfortunately, redundancy often sneaks in during this phase, disguised as stability or comfort. During descent, we might be in an old role that no longer challenges, a routine that has become monotonous, or a belief that once propelled forward but now feels like a burden. Yet, some fail to see this redundancy and continue living in their self-built pyramids.

A colleague once admitted, "I feel stuck. My role neither challenges me nor is required by the organisation, but I'm too afraid to move on." Many of us share this sentiment. The fear of change keeps us tethered to what feels safe, even when the safety net has frayed. Ironically, clinging to the familiar often costs many career professionals, and later, they regret it.

Breaking away from redundancy demands self-confrontation and courage. It means asking difficult questions: "Am I still contributing meaningfully, or am I hanging on, even though my organisation has moved on? What am I holding on to, and is it holding me back?" The answers may nudge us toward uncomfortable but necessary reflections—on letting go of roles, habits, or mindsets that no longer serve us in any manner except financial stability.

Stepping into the descent with intention is not about surrender but recalibration. Just as a snake sheds its old skin to allow growth, managing the descent means discarding what is redundant to uncover new opportunities for renewal. With clarity, this phase can be as enriching as the climb—perhaps even more so.

The descent is not about striving for more but aligning with what truly matters. So, here is a thought: What part of your career—or life—feels like an old skin you've outgrown? And are you ready to cast it off?

REFLECTION 1.12

OBSOLESCENCE: A SHADOW OF REDUNDANCY

"It is not the strongest of the species that survive, nor the most intelligent, but the most adaptable to change."
– Charles Darwin.

"Whatever exists is already becoming obsolete" is the Law of Obsolescence. As humans, we fit into this law so well that we begin to outgrow parts of ourselves and our environments as we age. We see obsolescence everywhere—in technology, socioeconomic practices, and even nature. Yet, we often nurture the belief that we are somehow exempt from this law. We resist change, even when experience tells us that change is inevitable. By doing so, we risk falling behind, defying Darwin's observation that "the most adaptable to change survives better than the strongest and smartest."

The human species is a testament to continuous change and evolution over millennia. The Buddhist doctrine of impermanence reminds us that nothing is permanent; even mountains erode and rivers change course. If the natural world adapts, why should we resist? Letting go of outdated notions, perspectives, beliefs, and dogmas is not just wise—it is necessary.

Redundancy inevitably gives way to obsolescence. To escape this, we must consciously recalibrate, realign, reinvent, renew, or even embrace personal rebirth. This is not just an option—it is a necessity. Life is dynamic, and so must we be. While change often occurs naturally, the key lies in being intentional about it—reading, learning, and experimenting to stay updated and relevant. Regular self-reinvention can transform routine progression into meaningful growth, saving us from the trap of irrelevance.

Many of us are entangled in repetitive routines, alternating between work, leisure, and mundane recreations. Comfortable as these routines may seem, they lead to obsolescence—a silent erosion of ourselves. Self-reflection, coupled with deliberate reinvention, is the Art of Survival.

Reinvention, however, comes with its challenges. It demands risk-taking and confronting our fears, especially the fear of failure. But here's the question: "What does failure truly mean to us?" The fear of failure is often exaggerated, while the benefits of taking risks are underestimated. Overcoming this mindset opens the door to growth and courage, enabling a more intentional and fulfilling life.

Staying relevant is not about chasing trends—it is about staying socially and emotionally fit.

Are you mindful of obsolescence silently shadowing your life? What steps can you take today to stay relevant and thrive in a world that never stops evolving?

REFLECTION 1.13

JOY – A SELF-FULFILLING PROPHECY OR REAL?

"Happiness is not something ready-made.
It comes from your own actions."
– Dalai Lama.

Whenever I meet retired colleagues, I often hear them say, "We're enjoying our time." This simple statement lingers in my mind. These people once held prestigious positions, made critical decisions, and enjoyed the privileges of professional success. Their titles opened doors, their influence shaped outcomes and their presence commanded respect.

So, what changed? Were they not experiencing joy during their careers despite the accolades and achievements? Or has their definition of joy evolved?

This paradox makes me question what joy truly means. Joy often seems tied to achievements, status, and recognition during our careers. Yet, in retirement, joy feels lighter—unburdened by targets, expectations, or the pressure to maintain an image.

It makes me wonder if joy in each phase of life is a self-fulfilling prophecy. Do we equate success with fulfilment during our careers because we are conditioned to? And later, in retirement, do we embrace contentment simply because it fits the narrative that retirement is meant for peace and joy?

A colleague once asked me, "Can we experience the freedom and contentment we associate with retirement while still actively working?" That struck me. Why not? Does joy have to wait for retirement, or can it be cultivated here and now, independent of titles, roles, or stages of life?

Perhaps we do not need to reinvent our understanding of joy but expand it. It can evolve with us if we root joy in purpose, gratitude, and fulfilling moments. Joy does not have to be tied to external achievements or milestones. Instead, it can be about finding meaning in the present, celebrating small victories, and being mindful of what truly matters.

So, let me ask: Are you chasing joy as something ready-made, creating it with your actions, or waiting for retirement to find it?

Reflection 1.14

THE UNPORTABLE SUCCESS OF CAREER TRANSITIONS

"What got you here won't get you there."
– Marshall Goldsmith, Author and Leadership Coach.

A long time ago, a Harvard Business Review article concluded that "competence and capability are not always portable." This insight has stuck with me because it perfectly encapsulates the paradox of career transitions: The skills and strategies that once ensured success in one role or industry do not always seamlessly translate into another.

Imagine stepping into a new "boxing ring." The rules have changed, the competitors are unfamiliar, and the strategies that once guaranteed victory might now fall flat. I have seen this firsthand. A leader transitions from the monopolistic public sector to the highly competitive private sector and feels disoriented. For him, the relentless demands of a market-driven environment replaced stability and predictability. Similarly, moving from a structured corporate role to a dynamic startup often requires abandoning meticulously honed systems for a culture that thrives on agility and experimentation.

Transitions like these are about adapting to new environments and recognising that old strengths can sometimes become barriers. Skills and habits that once propelled you forward might now hold you back. Career transitions demand learning new skills and unlearning those that no longer serve us.

I have heard colleagues speak of leaving their roles for "better opportunities," only to feel misaligned and stifled within months. Some even wished to return to their old positions. The issue was not their competence but the assumption that success could be universally replicated without accounting for the nuances of the new environment.

Here is the reality: stepping into a new role is not just a transition—it is stepping into a new arena. Like entering a boxing ring with unfamiliar fighters, each new role brings rhythm, unspoken rules, and unique dynamics. Success in this new space requires preparation—not just evaluating whether your skills match the demands, but whether your mindset is flexible enough to adapt to the unknown.

Marshall Goldsmith's advice reminds us that the strategies that brought us success in the past may not guarantee success in the future. When preparing for your next career move, ask yourself: How can I not only carry forward my strengths but also identify and embrace the new skills and mindset required to thrive in this unfamiliar boxing ring? Success is not just about what you bring—it is about how you adapt to what lies ahead.

And yes, as Darwin reminded us, adaptability remains the ultimate survival skill. Are you prepared to meet the demands of your next arena, or are you relying too heavily on yesterday's playbook?

REFLECTION 1.15

THE FALLACY OF DESIRES

*"It is not the man who has too little, but the man who craves
more, that is poor."*
– Seneca, Roman Stoic Philosopher.

The real challenge in life is not always about identifying what we lack; it is discerning what we genuinely want. We often confuse the absence of something with its necessity, falling into the fallacy that acquiring what we do not have will bring lasting contentment. This illusion can lead to relentless striving, distracting us from what enriches our lives.

Consider material possessions. A modest car priced at one million rupees meets its utility—safe, efficient transportation. A two-million-rupee car brings added comfort and perhaps a touch of social standing. But a twenty-million-rupee luxury vehicle often serves primarily as a status symbol. The question is, what are we really seeking? Is it utility and comfort, or are we chasing the fleeting satisfaction of social validation? When the lines blur, we risk pursuing desires misaligned with our true priorities, and the outcome is often an insatiable hunger for more.

Money is complex. Beyond its purchasing power and nominal value, it has a psychological weight shaped by the sacrifices made to earn it. For many, particularly those who have faced adversity, every rupee represents hours of effort, missed moments, and choices made. This emotional attachment can make spending difficult, even for meaningful purposes, as societal expectations nudge us toward indulgence that feels misaligned with the effort it took to accumulate that wealth.

It is not that ambition or desire are inherently wrong. The problem is how we define fulfilment. Are we chasing what truly matters or what the world convinces us we should want? Fulfilment does not lie in accumulating endlessly but in pausing to ask ourselves: What brings genuine joy? What aligns with our core values? When we untangle these questions, we shift from chasing illusions of wants and needs to pursuing what truly matters.

As I reflect on Seneca's words, I wonder: Are we poor because we lack what we desire or because our desires have made us blind to the riches we already hold?

What would change if your desires align with your deepest values rather than the fleeting illusions of what you think is missing?

REFLECTION 1.16

LIFE: A JOURNEY WITHOUT GUARANTEES

"Life is what happens to us while making other plans."
– Allen Saunders, American Journalist and Writer.

How often do we hear—or even say—"Nothing ever goes as expected"? But what are we really questioning? Are we blaming life itself or our response to its twists and turns? Life is not static; it unfolds through our choices, experiences, and expectations. When events do not align with our plans, we often resent the circumstances rather than reflecting on our own reactions.

Allen Saunders's words capture this truth: life comes with no guarantees. There's no promise of endless joy or immunity from pain. Gains and losses are inseparable—what feels like a setback today might reveal itself as a blessing tomorrow, while an achievement may later carry unforeseen costs. Life's unpredictability can be frustrating, but it makes it real and meaningful. Its charm lies in how it defies the scripts we write.

Society often amplifies our struggle by selling the illusion of guarantees. We are told that happiness, success, or security can be bought or achieved if we follow specific paths. These promises comfort but mislead us; life's essence lies in its fluidity. No one—not even ourselves—can guarantee outcomes.

Yet, we burden ourselves with expectations of certainty from a world that thrives on change. We cling to control, resisting life's inherent unpredictability. But the harder we try to master life, the more it reminds us that it does not work on our terms.

Perhaps the key is not about seeking guarantees but learning to embrace uncertainty. What if we flowed with life's twists and turns rather than resisting them? Gains and pains will come regardless of our efforts. Our task is not to eliminate uncertainty but to face it resiliently, steering through the unknown with trust in ourselves.

Life gives us the wheel, even if the ride is not smooth. How we steer determines the journey—not by chasing guarantees, but by embracing life as it unfolds.

What expectations do we hold about life's guarantees? How might letting go of these expectations free us to embrace their unpredictability and uncover new possibilities?

REFLECTION 1.17

THE GAIN WITHIN THE PAIN

"Out of suffering have emerged the strongest souls; the most massive characters are seared with scars."
– Kahlil Gibran.

"Life has been harsh." Building on the last reflection, is life truly harsh, or is it our perspective on what happens to us? Life is not an external force working against us—it is simply a series of events shaped by how we respond to them.

The pain we experience often hides the seeds of our most significant gains. We celebrate our successes as deserved, yet we see them as unfair when setbacks arise. It is strange, isn't it? Expecting only positive outcomes is like expecting a coin toss to always land on heads. Gains and pains are two sides of the same coin—inseparable, inevitable, and often interconnected.

I have seen this play out in my own life. Whenever I felt hurt or stuck in my career, I moved on and changed jobs. At the time, it felt like an uphill battle. But looking back, those moments of pain were the catalysts for some of my most significant learning and growth. Each change brought challenges but opened doors I had not imagined. Pain became the price of progress—a paradox I learned to embrace.

What is fascinating is how these experiences shift with perspective. A failure today might reveal itself as a stepping stone tomorrow, while a celebrated success might later show its hidden costs. Life does not give us guarantees—it offers us contrasts. Pain and gain are not opposites; they are part of the same journey.

So maybe life is not harsh—it is indifferent. Its challenges are not punishments but opportunities to grow, learn, and evolve. The key is how we respond—whether we let pain define us or use it to fuel our gains.

Think about a time when the pain seemed insurmountable. How did it shape you? Could it have been the starting point of a greater journey than you imagined?

CLOSING NOTE:
THE INNER JOURNEY: DEEPER ECHOES

Hear The Echoes and See The Patterns.

"Knowing yourself is the beginning of all wisdom."
– Aristotle.

The Echoes of Life is infinite, and I have only selected 17 reflections here. Our inner world is not a silent refuge; it is a chamber alive with echoes—the reverberations of struggles, insights, and questions that shape who we are and who we are becoming. Life, in all its intricacies, offers us a mirror—not just to reflect our image but to reveal the narratives we have embraced, the expectations we have pursued, and the truths we may have overlooked.

Through these 17 reflections, we have explored the depths of modern dilemmas, confronted the weight of emotional baggage, explored the timeless Flow of life, Career transitions, fallacies of desires and a few more. Each reflection reminds us that challenges are not merely hurdles but signposts, guiding us toward a more profound understanding. Self-reflection is not about definitive answers but about learning to live with meaningful questions— "What truly matters?"

As we step from the inner world into society, we enter a more vibrant and unpredictable realm—a kaleidoscope of shifting patterns and perspectives. Society's reflections on us are never fixed; they morph depending on our vantage point and the roles we assume. The key is to engage with society, which is constantly changing, as an active participant while holding onto our inner clarity, letting curiosity guide us rather than conformity dictate us.

KALEIDOSCOPIC SOCIETY: IN CONSTANT FLUX

"The only constant in life is change."
– Heraclitus, Greek Philosopher.

Society is like a kaleidoscope: It constantly changes, and every shift presents new patterns and perspectives shaped by the interplay of social, economic, religious, political, global, and technological forces. Heraclitus's insight perfectly encapsulates this dynamic: its ever-changing nature is the only certainty in society's evolution.

Yet, society is not passive; our collective actions, beliefs, and choices shape it. Our inevitable engagement with it creates tension—pressures that can inspire growth or leave us feeling constrained. Ignoring this tension risks losing sight of what matters, while thoughtful engagement transforms it into clarity and insight.

This section invites us to engage with and manage this tension. Instead of allowing society's flux to overwhelm us, we can use it as an opportunity to act intentionally and focus on what truly matters. By staying self-aware and reflective, we can distinguish meaningful patterns, shed what no longer serves us, and realign with our core values to take control of our journey.

REFLECTION 2.1

THE KALEIDOSCOPE OF CONTRADICTIONS

"No man ever steps in the same river twice, for it's not the same river, and he's not the same man."
– Heraclitus.

Heraclitus's words capture a profound truth about change: Time transforms everything—the river, the person, and their relationship. This interplay of time and change shapes individual experiences and society's rhythm.

I vividly recall being selected for my organisation's prestigious Golden Pot programme, a recognition of high potential. It felt like an undeniable affirmation of my abilities and future trajectory. Yet, when a promotion opportunity arose later, it went to someone else without explanation. The silence that followed felt personal, contradictory, and deeply frustrating.

Over time, however, I began to see the broader context. My earlier recognition reflected a moment when my contributions aligned perfectly with the organisation's priorities. When the promotion decision was made, those priorities shifted, and someone else's work resonated more with the organisation's evolving needs. What I had perceived as rejection was not a dismissal of my worth but a realignment of relevance—a shift dictated by time and context.

This experience mirrors the more significant dynamics of society. Like the river, society is a constantly evolving kaleidoscope reshaped by various forces. Its patterns shift with time, rewarding some while overlooking others—not because of inherent value or lack thereof, but because society's collective focus has moved. Acting as creator and critic, time turns objective truths into relative realities. Recognising this fluidity is liberating. In a society mainly indifferent to individual frustrations, understanding that contradictions stem from shifting priorities allows us to move beyond the immediacy of disappointment.

Heraclitus reminds us that life is never static. Time reshapes the river, the person, and their interaction. When we accept this, contradictions no longer feel like defeats—they become fleeting images cast by the kaleidoscope of change.

When contradictions seem unfair or disheartening, how can you step back to see them as transient patterns in life's kaleidoscope and use them to move forward?

REFLECTION 2.2

SOCIETAL CONSTRUCT: THE MAZE OF EXPECTATIONS

"When I let go of what I am, I become what I might be."
– Lao Tzu.

Expectations are intricately woven into society, shaping the roles we play and the paths we follow. While they offer structure and direction, they can also become invisible walls, confining us to a maze of societal pressures and inherited scripts. Some expectations push us toward growth, but others tether us to patterns that no longer reflect who we indeed are, keeping us from discovering ourselves.

Many of these expectations are passed down quietly, like family heirlooms; their origins are rarely questioned. As children, we absorb these narratives effortlessly. A student applauded for good grades may believe their worth depends on achievements. Another, taught to conform, may wear compliance as a badge of honour. Though helpful at times, these scripts can calcify into limiting beliefs if left unexamined, shaping our identity in ways we never consciously chose.

For me, the maze took the form of an aspiration to become a doctor—a dream that was not entirely mine but rooted in the hopes and expectations of those around me. When I did not achieve it, I felt an overwhelming sense of failing, as though I had let everyone down. I carried that weight for years until I realised the dream was not mine. By letting go of that inherited expectation, I found a path more aligned with my true self, bringing clarity and fulfilment.

But the maze is not confined to inherited expectations; it grows with daily demands. Societal norms and personal ambitions can motivate us to aim higher, but they can just as easily lead to burnout or disillusionment. Too much ambition can exhaust us, while too little can leave us feeling unfulfilled.

Over time, I have reframed my relationship with expectations. I have learned that not every expectation deserves to be carried. Success, I have come to understand, is not about meeting every demand or conforming to societal norms but about staying true to what matters most.

Lao Tzu's wisdom speaks directly to this journey: letting go is not about failure but transformation. When we release the roles and scripts that no longer serve us, we create space to become who we are meant to be.

What expectations—whether inherited or self-imposed—are you holding onto? Are they guiding you toward fulfilment, or have they become barriers to discovering your true self?

REFLECTION 2.3

PUPPETEERS AND PERCEIVED TRUTHS

"History is written by the victors."
– Winston Churchill.

Perceived truth often lies not in the facts but in how those facts are framed. Society's truths, like marionettes on strings, are shaped by the hands that hold power—its puppeteers. Leaders, influencers, and those in control of narratives decide what is celebrated and vilified and how events are remembered or erased.

I experienced this firsthand during a leadership transition in my organisation. A strategy once lauded as visionary and transformative suddenly became the subject of criticism. The facts had not changed; the outcomes were consistent. Yet, the narrative around them shifted, reflecting the perspectives and priorities of the new leadership. It was not the strategy that had failed—it was the hand holding the kaleidoscope that had changed.

This phenomenon is not confined to the corporate world. Consider political landscapes where policy decisions, once hailed as historic achievements, are later dismissed as misguided missteps under new leadership. The 2024 American presidential election is a prime example. Narratives around policies, successes, and failures shifted dramatically, not because the core facts evolved but because the individuals interpreting and communicating those facts changed.

Puppeteers wield immense influence over how society interprets events, decisions, and even people. Their strings—

the media, institutions, and public opinion—manipulate collective perceptions, creating a fluid and often fleeting sense of truth. Time amplifies this process, making what is celebrated today potentially ridiculed tomorrow, not because it was inherently right or wrong but because the context and storytellers have shifted.

This dynamic is not restricted to public spheres; it pervades personal and professional lives. How often have we seen someone's contributions viewed differently when a new manager or leader steps in? Successes are rebranded as failures or vice versa, depending on whose lens is applied. This is a shared experience that connects us all.

The puppeteers will always exist, pulling the strings and rearranging the patterns. The real question is: How can we remain true to ourselves when the truths around us are constantly shifting?

If history is written by the victors, who are writing our story? How do we identify the puppeteers shaping our narrative, and what steps can we take to reclaim control and stay true to our values?

REFLECTION 2.4

THE SILENT CHAINS OF APPROVAL

"He who has overcome his fears will truly be free."
– Aristotle.

"Impress the world." It is an unspoken rule, isn't it? This invisible expectation seems to guide us from the moment we are born. As babies, we are expected to charm, as students, to excel, and as adults, to win approval—from bosses, family, neighbours, and even gods. But why? Why do we get caught in this endless cycle of seeking approval?

Society thrives on conformity. It moulds us into predefined roles, ensuring predictability and control. We say what is expected, do what is acceptable, and believe what is convenient. Along the way, the pressure to belong often overshadows our individuality. This approval-seeking becomes so ingrained that we rarely pause to question it, mistaking it for the natural order of life.

Then there's fear—society's silent enforcer. Fear is not just an emotion anymore; it is a mechanism. Fear traders surround us—at home, at work, in politics, in the media, and even within ourselves. They thrive on uncertainties, feeding our anxieties about what might happen if we do not meet expectations or fit in. Over time, we internalise this fear, mistaking it for something innate. But think about it—were we born fearful, or did we learn to carry this burden?

Expectations, conformity, and fear work together to form invisible chains. We buy into fear and often trade away our peace, freedom, and authenticity. The fear of judgement, failure, or rejection can tether us to the approval of others, sometimes at the cost of who we indeed are.

But what if we paused to question these forces? Could fear simply be a tool of compliance rather than a natural truth? Perhaps living authentically is not about rebellion or rejection but about quietly redefining how we see ourselves. What do we value? What kind of life feels meaningful to us? Exploring these questions can shift the narrative from externally driven to internally guided.

Breaking free does not mean rejecting everything society offers. It is about discerning what aligns with our values and aspirations and letting go of what does not. Freedom might begin not with grand gestures but with small acts of trust in ourselves—our instincts, choices, and inner compass.

How much of our life is shaped by fear, conformity, or the need to impress others? What would it mean to let go of these chains and build a life guided by our values and aspirations?

REFLECTION 2.5

WEALTH: THE IDOL AND THE ENABLER

"It is not the man who has too little, but the man who craves more,
that is poor."
– Seneca.

Wealth. It is what we are all told to chase—the ultimate measure of success, a marker of security, and a gateway to comfort. But where is the line between necessity and excess? Financial stability is a sensible pursuit—it meets basic needs and builds a foundation for the future. Yet, when wealth shifts from a tool to a status symbol, it transforms into something else entirely: an idol.

This shift is not just personal; it is systemic. Consumerism thrives on the notion that more is better, convincing us that identity and success are tied to possessions. At the societal level, the disparity is stark: a small percentage of the population controls vast wealth, while billions struggle to secure necessities. This is not just about individual ambition—it is about a structure that rewards accumulation over equity.

Wealth, then, becomes a paradox. Admired, even revered, it is often hoarded or flaunted. Yet its true potential lies in its ability to uplift and create opportunities. History shows us that when voluntary redistribution fails, governments intervene—whether through progressive taxation or policies aimed at balancing the scales. Consider China's "common prosperity" push, a response to glaring inequality.

Frugality and purpose may offer a way forward. This is not about rejecting wealth but reframing its purpose.

What if wealth were seen not as a status measure but as a means to create equity, foster growth, and enable meaningful change? What if the measure of wealth was not how much one possesses but how effectively it is used to uplift others?

The question is not whether wealth is good or bad—it is neutral. Wealth's value lies in how we choose to wield it. When used wisely, wealth can empower, transform, and create opportunities. However, as an idol, it risks leaving us unfulfilled, no matter how much we accumulate. While societal systems perpetuate disparity, our individual choices collectively shape these systems. How we view and use wealth contributes to its broader impact.

Is wealth a tool in our lives, or has it become an idol? How might we redefine our relationship with wealth to enable purpose rather than status and accumulation?

REFLECTION 2.6

FAITH: A SOCIETAL PUSH?

"Faith is not something to grasp; it is a state to grow into."
– Mahatma Gandhi.

Faith often feels like an inheritance, doesn't it? We often absorb it through family, culture, and the world before we even understand it. At a Catholic university, I frequently heard students credit God for their successes—whether they aced an exam or hit a personal milestone. This made me pause and wonder: Where do their hard work, persistence, and effort fit into this narrative?

Faith, for many, is deeply personal. But it is impossible to ignore how society moulds it. Karl Marx described religion as an inversion of the material world, a way we attribute human effort and power to a divine entity. It is an interesting perspective—how much of what we believe comes from within, and how much is a reflection of societal expectations?

This societal push for faith becomes even more apparent when we examine organised religion. Institutions have commodified faith, turning it into an engine of influence and wealth. Religious structures flourish, while their followers often struggle to see the same prosperity. It is as though the institution thrives, but the individual gets left behind.

Yet, faith endures because it offers something essential—comfort and hope, especially in uncertain times. Saint Augustine captured this balance perfectly: "Pray as though everything depended on God. Work as though everything depended on you." Faith can guide us, but it is not a substitute for effort. Society's push to lean on faith shouldn't replace our ability to act.

Maybe it is time to rethink how we approach faith—not as something solely inherited or imposed, but as a personal choice. What if faith weren't about outsourcing responsibility to a higher power or a societal norm but finding strength in something bigger while staying grounded in our actions? Faith is not diminished by effort—it is enriched by it. I am sure God is not a cosmic vending machine or our micromanager. Perhaps faith is less about receiving and becoming—anchoring to a higher power for a breath in despair.

How has your faith been shaped—by personal experiences or societal expectations? How do you see faith and effort working together in your life?

REFLECTION 2.7

RELIGION IN THE AGE OF SCIENCE AND SCREENS

*"Faith is not clinging to a shrine but an endless
pilgrimage of the heart."*
*– Abraham Heschel, Jewish theologian, philosopher,
and civil rights activist.*

Why reflect on religion in a section about societal flux? Because religion, like society, is in constant transformation. For millennia, it has been humanity's compass—guiding behaviour, fostering community, and offering meaning amidst uncertainty. Yet today, in a world dominated by rapid technological advancements and shifting cultural paradigms, even this ancient compass appears to falter. How do we find direction when one of our oldest tools for navigating life seems increasingly out of sync with modern realities?

Religion thrived across ages because it served a purpose—it offered explanations for the inexplicable and provided a moral framework for coexistence. But as materialism, science, and technology reshape our worldview, their influence feels increasingly tenuous. Consider this: Pew Research reports that nearly 40% of U.S. Millennials identified as "Religious Nones" in 2019—a sharp rise from earlier decades. This shift is not merely a decline in rituals; it reflects a profound change in the spiritual landscape, driven by scepticism, disillusionment, and a focus on tangible, worldly goals.

The decline is compounded by how religion has been presented over the years. Narratives that once resonated now feel out of sync with a rational, evidence-driven era.

The commodification of faith—sacred spaces turned into tourist attractions and religion marketed as a commodity—has further eroded trust. Unsurprisingly, many turn instead to science, personal growth, or technological progress in their search for meaning.

But this is not about abandoning religion—it is about reimagining its role in an evolving world. Stripped of outdated veneers, religion still holds immense potential as a compass. A modern faith could embrace inclusivity by welcoming diverse perspectives and integrating scientific understanding. It could shift its focus from post-death promises to enriching life here and now, inspiring purpose, connection, and self-awareness in ways that resonate with today's generations.

The challenge is clear: reimagine religion not as a relic but as a dynamic guide for meaningful living. In a world in constant flux, we need anchors—not to hold us back but to help us steer. Religion, if it evolves, can still be one of those anchors.

What role does religion play in your life today? How might it evolve to serve as a meaningful compass in navigating the challenges of the modern world?

REFLECTION 2.8

THE FRAGILE INDIVIDUALISM

"Man is by nature a social animal."
– *Aristotle.*

Radical individualism has become a defining trait of our era, drawing both admiration and concern from philosophers, sociologists, and even institutional religions. It embodies the paradox of human progress: every gain carries an unforeseen cost. In this case, the price erodes the very bonds that make us human.

Aristotle's insight reminds us that humans are inherently social beings, designed to thrive in connection and community. Yet, have we become more like "solo animals" in our pursuit of autonomy and self-reliance? Collaboration, community, and shared purpose often resurface only in times of crisis or uncertainty. Otherwise, the trajectory seems clear: technology, materialism, and globalisation push us further into self-reliance, fraying the ties that once connected us, nature, and even ourselves.

What is driving this transformation? Some attribute it to materialism, globalisation, or the decline of faith in God and traditional institutions. Others see it as a natural outcome of a complex society prioritising individual achievement over collective well-being. Whatever the cause, the effects are undeniable: alienation, loneliness, and a fragmented sense of identity have become hallmarks of modern life.

The answer is not to abandon individualism but to temper it with the connection. Independence and self-expression are vital for personal growth but must coexist with collaboration and shared purpose. Humans are not meant to exist in isolation; even the most autonomous among us find meaning in relationships, shared goals, and a sense of belonging.

Rediscovering this balance does not require grand gestures. It begins with small acts of intentionality—reaching out to a friend, engaging in a local cause, or simply being present for those around us. By embracing independence and interdependence, we can mend the fragile fabric of our collective lives.

How has individualism shaped your life? What steps can you take to nurture meaningful connections while maintaining your independence?

REFLECTION 2.9

THE SILENT CLASH WITH NATURE

*"In the struggle against nature, man can only be victorious by
uniting with her."*
*– Friedrich Schiller, The Philosopher of
Freedom & Aesthetic Education.*

Humanity has always been in quiet conflict with nature—not out of malice, but out of necessity. From the earliest days of hunting and gathering to today's technological revolutions, we have sought to overcome nature's unpredictability: natural disasters, disease, and the inevitability of death. This struggle has shaped civilisations, driven innovation, and fuelled progress. Yet, as with all progress, it comes with unintended consequences.

Why do we strive to dominate nature? At its core lies fear—an acute awareness of our vulnerability. Unlike other species, humans are conscious of their mortality and fragility. This awareness, both a gift and a burden, compels us to master uncertainties. Yet, paradoxically, the more we attempt to conquer nature, the more alienated we become—from the natural world, each other, and even from a sense of inner balance.

Herein lies the paradox: humanity's most remarkable achievements have deepened its existential discontent. Nature's revolts—climate change, pandemics, and natural disasters—remind us of our limits. Despite all our progress, we cannot escape the fundamental truths of vulnerability and interdependence. Instead of finding peace in progress, we often feel destabilised, disconnected, and overwhelmed.

This disconnection manifests across society. Progress has created stark divisions—between those who benefit from advancements and those left behind, between humans and the environment, and even within ourselves. Our relationship with nature has become a zero-sum game: conquer or be conquered. But does domination have to be the only way forward?

The challenge lies in reconciliation. Progress does not need to mean estrangement, and power does not require equal control. Humanity's remarkable capacity for innovation and adaptation must be tempered with humility and acknowledging our place within the broader ecosystem. We are not masters of nature but an integral part of it. Accepting this truth is the first step toward moving beyond the illusion of supremacy. Only then can we strive for harmony with the world and ourselves.

In a world driven by progress, how can we find the humility to reconcile with nature and redefine our place?

REFLECTION 2.10

IS FREEDOM A FALLACY?

"Freedom is the will to be responsible for ourselves."
– Friedrich Nietzsche.

Is freedom just a platonic, metaphysical emotion—intuitive but rarely real? It is something I often wonder about. For centuries, humanity has fought for freedom with the same intensity as it has pursued materialistic pleasures. Wars have been waged, ideologies challenged, and revolutions sparked—all in the name of freedom. And yet, here is the paradox: even after centuries of struggle, have we ever truly gained the freedom to exercise our free will? Or is it always just a change of guard, a new set of rules to follow?

Freedom often arrives hand-in-hand with social controls. These controls—laws, norms, and expectations—are power tools in rulers' hands. Ostensibly meant to maintain order, they often end up as manipulation instruments. The irony is hard to miss: the systems created to preserve freedom frequently limit it. Regardless of their context—political, corporate, or religious—leaders draw enormous personal power from these controls, often forgetting that they are the very antithesis of the freedom they claim to champion.

But here is where it gets interesting. Freedom and self-control are often seen as opposites yet deeply intertwined. When self-control is lacking—whether in individuals or societies—social controls inevitably tighten. It is as if one fills the void left by the other. True freedom is not about the absence of rules but the ability to self-regulate. Societies and individuals who practice self-control can experience a lasting sense of freedom, while those who do not often find freedom slipping away, replaced by external constraints.

Is freedom, then, a fallacy? Perhaps not entirely, but it is not as absolute as it seems. It requires vigilance, not just in overthrowing external rulers or ideologies but in mastering ourselves. Without self-control, freedom risks becoming a distant ideal perpetually sought but rarely realised.

How does self-discipline shape your understanding of freedom? Can it help you find a balance between independence and the external controls of society?

REFLECTION 2.11

THE BURDEN OF TOO MANY CHOICES

"It is our choices that show what we truly are,
far more than our abilities."
– J.K. Rowling.

"Where there is no alternative, there is no problem," said American philosopher James Burnham. It is a profound observation, especially in today's world, where choices constantly surround us. On the surface, having many alternatives seems liberating, but more often than not, it becomes overwhelming. The abundance of options can create confusion, stress, and, ironically, dissatisfaction.

Here is the thing: with so many paths in front of us, society has turned missed opportunities into a constant refrain. We are told what we could have done differently from the moment we are born. You should have gone to that prestigious school, chosen that high-paying job, married someone from a wealthy family, or invested in that popular asset. It is a relentless narrative that seems like our lives are defined by the opportunities we have missed.

Not every opportunity is meant for us, and not every untaken path would have led to fulfilment. Regret often stems not from the choice itself but from the imagined outcome of the road untraveled.

But are these truly missed opportunities, or is it society's way of making us doubt our choices? Perhaps we are not perpetually missing out—possibly, opportunities are missing us, meaning they are not aligned with our true selves. After all, not every alternative is meant for us, and not every "missed" path would have been the right one. The more alternatives we consider, the more we risk creating unnecessary regret.

At its core, life often simplifies itself into binary choices: act or hesitate, love or resent, embrace or avoid. The alternatives become even fewer for those who follow a path of purpose or principle. When you're committed to being truthful, is dishonesty really an option? When you choose to embrace growth, is staying stagnant a real alternative? In such cases, the illusion of many choices, often stems from societal expectations, dissolves into a clarity of purpose.

Rather than being burdened by the illusion of missed chances, we can focus on our choices and the paths we are actively creating. Life is not defined by opportunities lost but by the ones we embrace. Regret fades when we recognise that not every door is meant to open for us and that the ones we walk through are the ones that truly matter.

How much of your life is shaped by the pressure of "missed opportunities"? How might reframing these moments as integral to your unique journey alter your perspective and bring you peace?

REFLECTION 2.12

NOT MY FAULT – THE BLAME ILLUSION

"You cannot control the wind, but you can adjust your sails."
– Anonymous.

"Not my fault. Events turned against me." How often have we heard this—or said it ourselves? It is a tempting escape, a way to deflect the discomfort of accountability. But pause for a moment: what role do events truly play in our failures? Events are constant, impartial, and universal. What truly matters is our response to them. Within that response lies our power to shape outcomes.

Imagine a sailor navigating stormy seas. The wind may blow fiercely, but it does not dictate the destination—the sailor does by adjusting the sails. Blaming the wind for being unfavourable does not change the course. The same principle applies to life: events may challenge us, but they do not control us. Our responses do.

This is not to suggest life is inherently fair or unfair. Events do not discriminate—they affect everyone, regardless of circumstance. Some may face more significant trials than others, but the principle remains the same: events do not fail us; we fail ourselves when we refuse to adapt. Excuses may sound convincing, but deep down, we know the truth. It is not the event that defeated us—it is the failure to rise and respond.

Consider Abraham Lincoln's life. Before becoming the 16th president of the United States, Lincoln endured numerous setbacks—job loss, business failures, and profound personal grief. Yet, he never blamed his circumstances. Instead, he adapted, learned, and persevered. His ability to "adjust his sails" in the face of relentless challenges defined his success and changed the course of history. His story is a powerful reminder of the transformative power of resilience and accountability.

The universe is indifferent, constantly presenting challenges to stimulate us. Without these trials, we risk stagnation. If we fail to act, we are not just blaming events; we are turning away from opportunities. The real question is not about what happened but what we did when it happened.

Have you recently attributed an outcome to external factors? How might the outcome have changed if you had taken responsibility for your actions and adapted accordingly?

REFLECTION 2.13

TIMING: AN IGNORED DIMENSION

"The meeting of preparation with opportunity generates the
offspring we call luck."
– Tony Robbins, World-renowned life coach and
Motivational speaker.

Being in the "right place at the right time" is often the secret to success. Many of us have witnessed this phenomenon—someone gets a promotion, lands a deal, or rises to a position of power seemingly by sheer luck. This universal pattern transcends industries, governments, corporations, media, and religious institutions. It makes us wonder: Is career success purely a result of timing, or is it earned through years of preparation and merit?

History suggests the answer is more complex. From presidents and prime ministers to business leaders and cultural icons, many have risen to prominence because they were in the right place at the right time. This is not limited to democracies or corporations—it is also visible in monarchies, dictatorships, and spiritual organisations. Timing often intersects with preparation but does not always discriminate between merit and mediocrity.

This reality can be frustrating for those who feel overlooked. It is disheartening to see mediocrity rewarded while others—often equally or more deserving—are left behind. But this is not just about fairness; it is about recognising how timing shapes societal narratives of success. Sometimes, chance occurrences elevate individuals not because they are the best but because they were present at a pivotal moment.

This observation is not meant to diminish the achievements of those who succeed. Many work tirelessly to be ready when the moment comes. But it is also a reminder for those who feel left behind: timing is not entirely in our control, and neither is societal judgement. What we can control is how we respond—by focusing on our own growth, staying prepared, and trusting that opportunities will arise that align with our unique journey.

Timing is not always fair, and it does not always reflect effort. However, understanding its role in shaping societal narratives allows us to navigate these realities with clarity and purpose. Life is not just about waiting for the "right place at the right time"; it is about being ready when that time comes.

Reflect on your personal experiences. When has timing influenced your achievements or failures? How could embracing its uncertainty allow you to concentrate on the aspects you can manage?

Reflection 2.14

RESULTS ARE ELASTIC – THE POWER OF EFFORT

"The only way to achieve the impossible is to believe it is possible."
– Charles Kingsleigh (A Fictional Character in Alice in
Wonderland 2010)

We often think of results as fixed, bound by our perceived capabilities. But here is the truth: results are elastic, stretching and expanding based on effort, commitment, and creativity. Record-breakers, innovators, and Mother Nature have repeatedly proven this universal reality.

Think of Michael Phelps, the most decorated Olympian in history. He did not start as a world champion. His success came from relentless effort, hours of training, and an unyielding belief in pushing the boundaries of human capability. Each new record he set was a testament to the elasticity of results—proof that hard work and persistence can redefine what is possible.

Consider the diligent farmer. The earth rewards their care with harvests far beyond the average. This is not luck—it is the elasticity of effort at work. Yet, we often underestimate this potential, bound by myths that limit what we think is possible. These self-imposed constraints act like invisible ceilings, keeping us from reaching our true capabilities. As Charles, the fictional character in Alice in Wonderland, comments: Impossibles are possible when we believe so.

Yet, we often underestimate this potential, bound by myths and self-imposed constraints that act like invisible ceilings. Human potential is infinite; the only limits are the ones we accept.

So why do so many of us cling to the idea that results are static? Perhaps it is fear of failure or the comfort of staying within known boundaries. But embracing the elasticity of effort means stepping beyond those fears. It is about realising that the harder we push, the more the world opens up.

Those who break free from these psychological barriers achieve the extraordinary, leaving others in awe. As the saying goes, fortune—and even the universe—favours the bold.

What limitations have you considered unchangeable in your life? How could a change in perspective or effort uncover new opportunities?

REFLECTION 2.15

FEAR TRADE – A MARKET OF ANXIETY

The only thing we have to fear is fear itself."
– Franklin D. Roosevelt.

"Fear sells." It is a simple truth but it has grown into a vast industry today. Fear is no longer just an emotion; it is a global commodity traded in trillions of dollars by governments, corporations, the media, and even individuals. Entire systems thrive on exploiting fear, turning it into a product to sell, an emotion to manipulate, and a tool to control. The worst part? We have become willing buyers, trading our peace of mind for narratives that amplify uncertainty and doubt.

Fear traders are omnipresent. Turn on the news, and crises dominate the headlines. Politicians use fear to sway opinions and secure votes. Social media algorithms amplify anxiety, feeding on our engagement with negativity. Even closer to home, fear manifests subtly in overbearing expectations, workplace pressures, and societal norms that confine rather than liberate. Fear is not merely a consequence of these systems; it is the fuel that powers them, intentionally cultivated to maintain control and drive profits.

But were we always this fearful? As children, we were born fearless—curious, daring, and unafraid to explore. Fear was not inherent; it was learned. Over time, we internalised it, influenced by those around us and the systems we inhabit. The fear traders thrive on this learned vulnerability, keeping us tethered to their narratives.

Breaking this cycle demands awareness. Fear thrives in uncertainty and inflated expectations. Recognising these triggers allows us to reclaim control and discern when fear is real and a narrative designed to manipulate us. Ancient wisdom, like the Vedantic principles of selflessness and righteousness, offers tools to transcend fear. By grounding ourselves in purpose and authenticity, we can detach from fear's grip and reconnect with the courage we once knew innately.

When fear arises, pause and reflect. Is it a genuine signal of danger or someone else's tool to influence you? By asking this question, we reclaim our power and begin to unlearn the fears we have absorbed. Liberation is not about eliminating fear but choosing not to let it define us.

How much of the fear you experience is truly your own? What steps can you take to discern authentic fears and those sold to you—and regain your peace?

REFLECTION 2.16

THE PANDEMIC OF GREED

"There is a sufficiency in the world for man's need but not for man's greed."
– Mahatma Gandhi.

Why do accomplished, intelligent, and ethical leaders sometimes stumble into the quagmire of corporate fraud? It is a question that is both puzzling and telling. These individuals, celebrated for their discipline and achievements, often falter—not because of personal failings alone but because of a much larger force: collective greed.

Greed has become the silent driver of modern societies. What starts as ambition often escalates into a culture of relentless pursuit, where profits overshadow principles. This is not just about individual choices—it is about systems that reward overconfidence, misjudgment, and short-term gains, creating a whirlpool that pulls even the most grounded leaders into its depths.

But here is the bigger picture: greed is not confined to corporations. It has transcended boundaries and become a societal epidemic. Like a pandemic, it infects every corner—governments, businesses, communities, and even individuals. The desire for wealth, power, and control creates inequalities, destabilising societies and turning potential progress into moral disasters.

Consider the financial crises of recent decades. They were not isolated incidents. They were the product of systemic greed—a cascade of decisions where profit trumped prudence.

The 2008 financial crisis, for instance, was not just about reckless lending or risky investments; it was a collective failure where institutions, leaders, and entire systems prioritised self-interest over stability. The ripple effects were not just economic; they were social, eroding trust and deepening divides.

And it is not just institutions. Greed has become normalised even at an individual level. We have turned accumulation into an aspiration, and greed is celebrated as ambition.

The irony is that greed never fulfils its promise—it demands more. It promises progress but often delivers inequality and distrust. If we continue to normalise greed as ambition, we risk eroding the very foundations of our societies. The challenge is not just recognising greed; it is actively choosing to prioritise fairness, ethics, and shared growth. True progress is not measured by how much we accumulate but by how much we contribute to collective well-being. Only then can we redefine success for individuals, organisations, and society.

How often do we mistake greed for ambition, both individually and collectively? What would change if we measured success not by accumulation but by the value we create for others?

REFLECTION 2.17

EMOTIONAL EQUITY – THE SOUL OF SOCIETIES

"Compassion is the currency that leads to true wealth."
– Jim Carrey, Canadian Actor.

When crises strike, they expose vulnerabilities and reveal the unseen forces that bind us. COVID-19 was a powerful reminder of one such force—emotional equity, the deep well of empathy, trust, and solidarity that holds societies together when external resources seem insufficient.

Emotional equity manifested unexpectedly in the face of unprecedented challenges. People and communities—often those with the least to give—extended kindness, shared resources, and worked together to overcome barriers. Small businesses retooled to support healthcare needs, neighbours checked in on one another, and individuals offered their time and energy to help those in need. This was not about transactional charity—it was a collective expression of humanity, where giving and receiving became an ongoing, mutual exchange that transcended material wealth.

This mutual exchange is the philanthropy of reciprocity but with a focus on connection rather than a simple act of giving. The true power of reciprocity emerged through grand gestures and simple, everyday acts—moments when communities and individuals came together, not as separate entities, but as parts of a collective whole. What made these acts significant was the emotional investment behind them, the genuine concern for the well-being of others, which fuelled a cycle of support and care.

Like any true asset, emotional equity grows stronger the more it is shared. In times of crisis, this equity allows societies to withstand adversity. Yet, this emotional strength is often invisible in times of normalcy, overshadowed by the focus on material progress. The paradox lies in how easily this valuable resource can be overlooked in calmer times. How do we sustain the spirit of generosity and mutual care when the urgency of the crisis fades?

As I reflect, I realise that while governments and organisations could offer aid and relief packages, they were not enough to carry societies through the crisis. Emotional equity—trust, compassion, and shared purpose—allowed people to adapt and persevere. These moments taught us that a society's strength is not defined solely by its resources but by its emotional fabric—the collective spirit that weaves its people together.

This pandemic showed us that emotional equity is the cornerstone of resilience. It is the soul of societies, enabling us to rise above our challenges and emerge stronger. If we can nurture this asset, we can create a foundation supporting our survival and ability to thrive, even when external circumstances change.

What acts of emotional equity have you experienced or witnessed in your life? How can you contribute to nurturing this invisible yet powerful resource in times of crisis and every day?

REFLECTION 2.18

THE ETERNAL CONFLICT: SEEKING PEACE THROUGH WAR

"Wars are poor chisels for carving out peaceful tomorrows."
– Martin Luther King Jr.

The conflict has been part of our story since the beginning. Remember Cain and Abel? In the Biblical tale, Cain killed his brother without reason or mercy. This makes you wonder: Is violence hardwired into the fabric of creation?

Fast forward to 12,000 years ago—hunters warring with farmers—and not much has changed. Battles, big and small, have marked every century. So, why are we like this? Is it about identity? Supremacy? The need to feel secure? Or maybe, deep down, there's something darker—a kind of "bloodlust" we do not fully understand.

As individuals, we crave peace. But as groups, we are often drawn to war. And it is not just one civilisation or belief system to blame. Secular and Socialistic nations, theocracies, dictators—everyone has had their hand in it. Wars for land, for power, for ideology... the reasons change, but the devastation does not.

Take religion, for instance. Over time, the "Kingdom of God" became the rallying cry for countless battles. Heaven—something no one could even prove—was used as the ultimate motivator for armies. And yet, history shows us that empires built on violence, whether by religious crusaders or warlords like Genghis Khan, do not last. They crumble. It seems nature itself does not tolerate systems that thrive on destruction and are antithetical.

And yet, in every war, there's a strange irony: the promise of peace. Leaders, kings, and ideologues sell war as the ultimate solution to the conflict. The "greater good" is used to justify violence, often in the name of protection, justice, or divine will. But can peace born of violence ever last? History suggests otherwise. Destruction, even when well-intentioned, carries the seeds of its undoing.

So, is peace from conflict just an illusion? Or could it be that peace isn't born from war but from how we respond to conflict? Perhaps the answer lies not in choosing violence but in redefining the systems, ideologies, and beliefs that perpetuate it. True peace requires not victory but understanding—a deliberate effort to resolve the fears, insecurities, and divisions that drive us to war in the first place.

What fears or beliefs drive humanity to choose war over dialogue? How might embracing understanding over dominance transform how we approach global and personal conflict?

CLOSING NOTE: EMBRACING FLUX: THE RHYTHM OF PROGRESS

"Chaos is inherent in all compounded things. Strive on with diligence."
– Buddha.

Among many saints and philosophers, Buddha emphasised the impermanent nature of the world—a truth mirrored in society's kaleidoscope. Should we be worried? Not at all. This flux has been society's nature since antiquity. As Aristotle called us, humans are rational animals, and the onus is on us to rationalise, respond, and adapt accordingly. But is it that simple? Yes, if we exercise our agency responsibly!

The reflections in part 2 revisited the many ways society tries to pull us into its realm through fear, greed, choices, and expectations. Yet they also remind us that we are not powerless while societal forces influence us. If we understand society's kaleidoscopic nature, we can move beyond being passive spectators and actively safeguard our values and interests.

As we close this chapter on society, we focus on a microcosm within it: the corporate world. Here, the dynamics shift, but the influence of societal forces remains strong.

In the reflections in part 3, we'll tread the corporate jungle and explore stories of success breeding arrogance, loyalty becoming a trap, and the pursuit of progress leading us away from our core. No one is exempt from these forces—you may find echoes of your experiences in the stories ahead.

Rest assured, self-reflection will act as your compass, guiding you back to the path you may have lost in the jungles!

Part 3.0

CORPORATE JUNGLE: LOST PATHS

"The truth is rarely pure and never simple."
– Oscar Wilde.

Paradoxes thrive beneath the surface and in the deep layers of the corporate world. While organisational charts, vision statements, and mission statements suggest clarity, the reality is far more complex. Corporations are not simply entities of structure and strategy but dynamic microcosms reflecting the contradictions and complexities we encounter within ourselves and society.

The corporate journey is not just about climbing ladders or meeting targets—it is a maze of unwritten rules, power dynamics, and competing priorities. It tests our values, perceptions of success, and commitment to values. Leadership decisions can inspire and alienate. This is the arena where success can breed both arrogance and humility. Even loyalty—a celebrated virtue—can transform into a trap.

This section delves into these contradictions, illuminating the corporate jungle's hidden paths, unseen traps, and fragmented truths. The reflections ahead explore what it means to travel this terrain with clarity, integrity, and self-awareness. We uncover lessons that resonate far beyond the boardroom by dissecting the tension between personal authenticity and organisational demands.

As we step into the corporate jungle, let us carry forward the tools we have sharpened—introspection and a willingness to question. Amidst the facades, we seek to succeed and thrive intact without compromise.

REFLECTION 3.1

THE DILEMMA OF THE MANY FACES OF CULTURE

*"Your vision will become clear only when you can
look into your heart."*
– Carl Jung.

Starting a new job often feels like venturing into uncharted waters. You're learning the ropes of your role and trying to survive the organisation's culture. But what happens when that culture feels undefined, fragmented, or contradictory?

I faced this question when I joined a company in a different sector. To prepare, I asked a friend who had worked there, "What is the company culture like?"

His reply caught me off guard: "It does not have a culture."

Perplexed, I pressed further: "How can a company not have a culture?"

His explanation revealed an unexpected challenge: "It is still figuring itself out. They have hired people everywhere—private companies, the public sector, government. Everyone brings their way of working, and it is chaotic."

It felt like stepping into a hall of mirrors, with every reflection revealing something different. Despite the ambiguity, I decided to join, drawn by the promise of growth. Once inside, it became clear that the culture was not one cohesive whole; it was fragmented. Each team operated as a fiefdom, carrying the norms and values of its members and the boss's past workplaces. The result was a landscape of clashing values, processes, and expectations.

Colleagues who joined around the same time mirrored my experience. Some chose to adapt quietly, blending into the chaos. Others aligned with a particular group, finding a sense of belonging. I, however, stood at a crossroads, questioning which version of the organisation was real.

Amidst this uncertainty, it struck me: I was so busy decoding the external mirrors that I would forgotten to look into my own. What were my principles? What kind of leader did I want to be in this setting?

This shift in focus—turning to my inner mirror—was transformative. Instead of being consumed by external chaos, I grounded myself in what mattered most. I realised that clarity does not come from choosing the "right" reflection but from trusting one's own.

Organisations, like mirrors, reflect fragments of reality. The real challenge is knowing when to decode them and when to turn inward, reconnecting with one's core values to navigate the complexity.

How often do you pause to reconnect with your inner mirror when faced with a fragmented culture? What steps can you take to anchor yourself amidst the chaos?

REFLECTION 3.2

ALIGNMENT WITH THE BOSS: IMPERATIVE OR ILLUSION

"Blind loyalty makes room for manipulation."
– Anonymous.

Here is a corporate reality that often goes unspoken: while organisations publicly celebrate performance, creativity, and innovation, what they frequently reward is something else entirely—loyalty to authority.

I have experienced this firsthand. In one of my roles, my boss said, "You're not in my group." It was not about my performance or contributions but about alignment. In another instance, a Managing Director casually remarked to the HR Head, "He isn't loyal to me." These moments made me question whether loyalty to an individual is more important than genuine contributions.

Organisations often tout meritocracy, but beneath the surface lies an unspoken truth: aligning with power frequently takes precedence over authentic results. A subtle yet pervasive undercurrent shapes promotions, decisions, and careers in ways that meritocracy claims to prevent.

Here is the irony: aligning with authority can sometimes work in your favour. It offers security and creates the illusion of being "in the loop." But at what cost? You're expected to realign with the new leader when your boss changes. How many times can one realign? How many compromises must one make? This cycle can be stifling, leaving little room for innovation, fresh ideas, or diversity of thought. Balancing loyalty with your identity is not easy, but staying aligned with your moral compass is essential.

Upon reflection, I have realised that loyalty is not inherently harmful. Alignment is necessary for collaboration and achieving a shared vision. However, loyalty loses its purpose when it becomes a tool to maintain power structures rather than further the organisation's mission. Instead, it becomes another "mirror" to interpret—similar to the fragmented reflections of corporate culture I encountered earlier.

So, how do we manage? The key is to question whether this alignment serves the greater good or perpetuates existing hierarchies. Balancing loyalty with authenticity is not easy, but remaining faithful to ourselves and our work is essential.

Have you faced moments where loyalty to authority overshadowed performance? How did you manage the situation, and what steps can you take to balance alignment with authenticity in your professional journey?

REFLECTION 3.3

INCOMPETENCE ASCENDS, WHEN SYCOPHANCY RULES

"Flattery is like cologne water, to be smelt, not swallowed."
– Josh Billings, Pen name of Henry Wheeler Shaw, an American humorist, Writer, and Lecturer.

Have you ever wondered how some leaders rise to the top despite incompetence? This phenomenon feels like the corporate version of defying gravity; its fuel is sycophancy.

Darwin's "survival of the fittest" once seemed to define success—grit, intelligence, and perseverance ruled. But today's corporate world sometimes operates on a different principle: "success of the sycophant." Incompetence does not just survive; it thrives on flattery and subservience rather than merit or effort, threatening the health of the Corporate world.

Once incompetence reaches leadership levels, it does not just stop there—it reinforces itself. Incompetent leaders tend to surround themselves with people who mirror their perspectives and avoid challenging their authority. This creates an echo chamber, stifling creativity and sidelining dissent. Over time, the organisation suffers as mediocrity becomes the norm and competence is pushed to the margins.

How does sycophancy gain such a foothold? It thrives on aligning with power, not the purpose. Sycophants glorify superiors, feed their egos, and avoid uncomfortable truths. This might create an illusion of loyalty and stability but undermines trust and objectivity. Worse, it discourages honest feedback, leaving organisations blind to their weaknesses.

The real dilemma is countering this culture. Organisations must prioritise merit, transparency, and constructive dissent over personal loyalty. Leaders must actively seek out diverse perspectives, value honest criticism, and resist the allure of flattery. It is difficult—challenging sycophancy requires a cultural shift—but it is essential for organisational health and integrity.

We must ask ourselves: Are we loyal to individuals or the organisation's purpose? When sycophancy goes unchecked, it erodes trust and weakens the foundation of progress.

Have you observed situations where sycophancy replaced competence in decision-making? What steps can you take as a leader or team member to foster a culture prioritising integrity and constructive dissent over flattery?

REFLECTION 3.4

THE RIPPLE EFFECT: WHEN DECISIONS GO BEYOND THE BOARDROOM

"You are free to make choices, but you are not free from the consequences of those choices."
– Anonymous.

Have you ever been in a meeting where a decision seemed flawless on paper—logical, data-driven, and perfectly aligned with strategy—only to watch it ripple out in ways no one anticipated? This is the paradox of corporate decision-making: choices made with the best intentions often lead to unintended consequences, sometimes far removed from their original purpose.

Consider high-profile incidents like oil spills contaminating coastlines, factory closures displacing entire communities, or data breaches compromising customer trust. These disasters did not start as bad decisions. They likely began as well-meaning plans: cost-saving measures, operational efficiency drives, or strategies for-profit growth. But spreadsheets do not tell the whole story. They do not capture the livelihoods lost, ecosystems damaged, or trust eroded when things go wrong.

I recall a pivotal moment in a boardroom when a factory closure was proposed to cut costs. The rationale was sound on paper, but someone asked a crucial question: "What about the families who depend on this factory? What happens to them?" That question lingered with me. Though valid, it was brushed aside in favour of "bigger priorities." The factory closed, and the company saved money, but the ripple effects devastated a community for years.

No leader sets out to create harm. Most decisions genuinely aim for the greater good. Yet the relentless pressure to deliver results—whether for shareholders or quarterly targets—can obscure the broader impact. The real test of leadership arises when unintended consequences emerge. Do we face them, take responsibility, and adapt? Or do we choose to ignore them, hoping they will resolve themselves?

This is the challenge of leadership: balancing strategy with accountability. It demands looking beyond data and asking hard questions like, "Who will this decision impact?" and "How do we achieve our goals while minimising harm?" Great leaders do not shy away from these questions—they embrace them, understanding that success is not just measured in profits, integrity, and responsibility.

Have you experienced unintended consequences from a decision? How did you address them, and what did you learn about balancing results with accountability?

REFLECTION 3.5

DUALITY OF CORPORATE DECISIONS

"There are no facts, only interpretations."
– Friedrich Nietzsche.

Isn't it fascinating how the same decision can appear entirely different depending on where you stand? I recall a challenging market scenario involving domestic producers and imports. Our team managed significant product volumes, and mounting import pressures threatened local producers. Seeking tariff protection seemed like the logical solution.

From one perspective, it was a triumph. Domestic producers hailed us as their champions, safeguarding their survival in a challenging climate. The numbers reinforced this narrative—we maintained operating rates, protected jobs, and preserved industrial capabilities.

But from another perspective, the story looked entirely different. Consumers faced higher prices and fewer choices, leading them to view our actions as restrictive rather than protective. The same decision painted two conflicting pictures, each valid within its context.

It reminded me of Schrödinger's Cat—a thought experiment in quantum physics. In this paradox, a cat in a sealed box is both alive and dead until someone opens the box and observes it. Similarly, our decision was both protective and restrictive, depending on who was impacted by it and from what perspective.

This experience reshaped how I approach decisions. Instead of asking, "Was this right or wrong?" I began asking, "Right or wrong, for whom?" Like light, does truth have a dual nature? Its essence seems to shift depending on the lens through which it is seen.

This duality is not confined to business. Truth often manifests in multiple realities in leadership, relationships, and personal choices. Should we strive to reduce these complexities to a single truth or perspective, or should we seek to understand and respect the coexistence of multiple viewpoints?

How often do you consider opposing perspectives when making decisions? What steps can you take to balance conflicting truths and honour the nuances they bring?

REFLECTION 3.6

BALANCING THE SCALES: ETHICS VS. PROGRESS

*"The selfish ends you serve will take you no further than yourself.
The ends you serve that are for all will take you into eternity."
– Marcus Garvey, Jamaican-born political leader, orator,
entrepreneur, and activist, best known for Pan-Africanism.*

Corporate life often feels like a relentless race. Whether it is about meeting quarterly targets, cutting costs, or expanding into new markets, decisions are frequently judged by their immediate results. But what happens when this race comes at a price that forces us to ask deeper questions about fairness, sustainability, and humanity?

Take the mass layoffs during the COVID-19 pandemic. Downsizing was often framed as a survival strategy—essential to ensure the organisation's continuity. While the financial logic behind these decisions was clear, the human cost was immense. Families faced instability, communities were disrupted, and the trust between employees and employers was deeply eroded. Was this truly the only option?

Similarly, consider diversification as a strategy. A company I knew ventured into IT-enabled services during an industry boom. On the surface, this was a forward-thinking move. But without alignment with the company's strengths or proper groundwork, the effort floundered. Resources were wasted, employees were let go, and what began as a pursuit of progress ended in futility. Responsibility took a backseat, even as the organisation paid the price for its misjudged ambition.

Even automation, often celebrated as the pinnacle of innovation, has ethical paradoxes. While it undoubtedly boosts productivity and reduces costs, it frequently displaces workers and undermines community stability. While not inherently wrong, these decisions reveal the underestimated human and societal costs of pursuing efficiency.

The deeper challenge lies in redefining progress. It must extend beyond immediate results to include considerations of long-term impact and the well-being of those affected. Ethical leadership requires pausing to ask critical questions: Who will this decision affect? How do we minimise harm while pursuing progress?

Leadership is not just about delivering results; it is about ensuring those results align with ethical standards. Leaders must embrace long-term thinking by integrating ethical considerations into progress measures, ensuring their decisions leave a lasting positive impact on all stakeholders.

Have you faced a moment where achieving results conflicted with your values? Looking back, what might you have done differently to balance progress with responsibility?

REFLECTION 3.7

CORPORATE VALUES: A DICHOTOMY OF OPTICS AND ACTIONS

"Corporate values are like quantum particles—dual in nature, appearing solid in the handbook but wavering in the boardroom."
– Inspired by the quantum theories of Louis de Broglie and Niels Bohr.

Corporate truth is rarely absolute; it is dynamic, opaque, and shifts depending on the observer. Organisations proudly declare values like transparency, fairness, and sustainability, yet these ideals often shine more brightly in employee handbooks and ethics policies than in strategic decisions. The tyranny lies in how rigorously these values are applied to individuals, even as they quietly disappear in the face of market strategies or quarterly goals.

Consider sustainability as a corporate value. Many companies advocate environmental responsibility, urging employees to reduce waste or embrace sustainable practices. Yet, these organisations might expand operations into fragile ecosystems or lobby for relaxed environmental regulations. This dichotomy—between the principles expected of individuals and the leniency allowed for organisational behaviour—creates a disconnect between words and actions.

The predicament becomes even sharper during economic crises. Downsizing, justified as "necessary," is seen even in companies that claim to prioritise people. Automation strategies, while efficient, can displace workers and destabilise communities, undermining long-term societal harmony. These moments reveal how corporate values can be as fluid as aspirational, bending to align with immediate priorities rather than guiding consistent action.

Adding to the complexity is the crafting of external narratives. Leaders meticulously shape images that project alignment with declared values, but boardroom realities often diverge. Strategies may be framed to reflect ethical ideals, yet execution frequently undermines them. This performative aspect of corporate values—what appears versus what is—can erode trust within and outside the organisation.

The real challenge is moving values beyond optics. Ethical leadership lies in embracing the dichotomies of corporate values and making decisions that reflect core principles, even when inconvenient. It is not about erasing contradictions but confronting and resolving them to align actions with declared ideals.

Have you witnessed corporate values being used more for optics than genuine action? What tangible steps can leaders take to bridge the gap between declared values and consistent behaviours, fostering trust and integrity throughout the organisation?

REFLECTION 3.8

THE GOLD FENCING: RETENTION OR RESTRICTION?

"Comfort is the enemy of progress."
– P.T. Barnum, American showman and Entrepreneur.

Have you ever encountered the predicament of professional rewards? Enticing pay packages, prestigious titles, and promises of stability are often celebrated as milestones of career success. Yet, these very rewards can evolve into constraints—what seemed like a golden opportunity becomes a ring-fenced existence, trapping individuals and organisations in cycles of potential redundancy and inbreeding.

Ring-fencing strategies—such as stock options that vest over a long period, bonuses tied to tenure, or specialised roles that limit exposure to other business areas—can have unintended consequences for employees. The longer they stay, the narrower their career options may become unless they progress vertically. They may feel indispensable within their current role but seldom realise that they are increasingly turning "unemployable" in their organisations and elsewhere, their skills tailored too narrowly to one organisation's needs. What began as a pathway to recognition becomes a gilded cage.

For corporations, these strategies often serve dual purposes. They retain top talent while simultaneously preventing their competition from accessing critical expertise. The downside of such tactics can also breed complacency—retention strategies focusing more on blocking competitors than fostering growth risk, underemployment and lowered productivity.

The impact is profound on both sides. Employees who cling to comfort may miss opportunities for renewal and progression, and their enthusiasm for work is slowly fading. Organisations that cling to talent for continuity may struggle to innovate or respond effectively to market shifts, and eventually, they may find the employees a liability.

Breaking this cycle requires rethinking what it means to thrive. For employees, this means asking: Am I fulfilling my purpose here or merely staying comfortable? For organisations, it means striking a balance between the value of retention and the need for fresh perspectives and adaptability.

When does security stop fostering growth and start limiting it? How can organisations and individuals collaborate to ensure retention strategies unlock potential instead of confining it? What has been your experience?

REFLECTION 3.9

THE CORPORATE CATCH-22

"Chains of gold are still chains."
– Anonymous.

Big pay cheques and prestigious titles are corporations' golden tickets to ring-fence talent. At first glance, this strategy seems like a win-win: Employees gain security and recognition, while organisations retain critical resources. However, this approach often backfires in the context of mergers and acquisitions, turning retained talent into an unintended liability.

I have seen how this dynamic plays out in corporate acquisitions. Gold-caged employees—those lured into roles with hefty compensation packages—often struggle during mergers. Having spent years immersed in the culture and systems of their original organisations, they may become overly comfortable or pampered. When a new organisation takes over, these employees often find themselves sidelined, their roles diminished, and their contributions undervalued. What follows is a workforce that feels out of place, disengaged, and demoralised.

From the organisation's perspective, this creates the ultimate catch-22. The very talent they have worked hard to retain can become a chokepoint, blocking progress by occupying roles that no longer align with the company's evolving needs. Despite their experience, these employees may find their specialisation limiting, eventually being perceived as "unemployable" within and beyond the organisation.

For employees, the dilemma is equally daunting. Rewards that once symbolised achievement can transform into shackles. The longer they stay, the more challenging it becomes to leave. Adapting to a new environment and unfamiliar cultures and proving one's value again can feel like a mountain to climb, especially for those accustomed to comfort and familiarity.

While ring-fencing strategies might provide short-term stability, they often create long-term challenges for organisations and employees. This raises a pressing question: Are these practices sustainable or merely delaying inevitable transitions?

The solution lies in rethinking retention. Organisations must recognise that keeping talent is not enough—they must also enable talent to grow. Fostering adaptability, encouraging cross-functional learning, and aligning roles with evolving goals can turn potential chokepoints into drivers of renewal.

The key for employees is embracing personal growth. This means stepping beyond familiar boundaries, seeking diverse experiences, and cultivating curiosity about change. No matter how ornate, a gold cage remains a cage—unless one dares to step out.

How can organisations transform retained talent into bridges for growth rather than barriers in mergers and acquisitions? And for employees, how can you build the mindset and skills to thrive in uncertain landscapes?

REFLECTION 3.10

DILEMMA OF STABILITY VS. DIVERSIFICATION

"The art of progress is to preserve order amid change and to preserve change amid order."
– Alfred North Whitehead, a British Mathematician known for Process Philosophy.

The interplay between stability and diversification is one of the most profound challenges in corporate strategy. Stability provides trust, consistency, and a sense of purpose—the foundation that keeps an organisation grounded. Diversification, in contrast, opens doors to growth, evolution, and relevance in a competitive world. These forces are not opposites but complementary, each essential to progress when approached with intention.

Ignoring the delicate balance between stability and diversification can lead to significant risks. I have witnessed this firsthand in a company I worked for. Seduced by the rapid growth of the ITES sector, the company ventured boldly into this new territory. I have shared this example earlier too. The potential was undeniable—higher valuations, increased market capitalisation, and heightened shareholder interest. However, the effort faltered. The company's core strengths did not align with the demands of this new space. This misstep underscored a critical truth: diversification must be grounded in preparation and aligned with an organisation's foundation.

On the other hand, I have seen businesses resist diversification entirely, holding tightly to what has always worked. Their belief in the strength of legacy systems and the conviction that their business models were unshakeable truths made them hesitant to explore new opportunities. However, as customer needs evolved and competitors adapted, their stability stagnated. This reluctance to diversify proved risky and, in some cases, fatal.

Customers often hold the key to the success of diversification. They act as the final judges, determining whether a new product or strategy meets their needs. Yet, organisations can become insular, crafting plans that excite internally but fail to connect with external realities. Adequate diversification is not just about pursuing trends— it is about creating something meaningful, rooted in a deep understanding of the customer's evolving expectations.

The duality of stability and diversification does not demand a choice but rather a balance to ensure the organisation remains competitive and future-ready. Corporate leaders must reflect deeply, act decisively, and remain open to questioning long-held assumptions. Achieving this balance is not easy, but it is essential for sustaining in the long run.

Have you experienced moments where the need for stability clashed with the drive to diversify? How did you navigate these tensions, and what insights did you gain about achieving balance?

REFLECTION 3.11

THE MISALIGNMENT OF SCALE AND VISION

"Growth for the sake of growth is the ideology of the cancer cell."
– Edward Abbey, American author, Essayist,
and Environmental activist.

Edward Abbey's words challenge us to reflect deeply on our pursuit of scale. Does it serve a meaningful purpose, or is it an empty measure of success?

Scale and vision—are two concepts often intertwined in leadership narratives. We celebrate leaders who expand their organisations, dominate markets, and shatter revenue records, equating size with visionary success. But is scale truly the hallmark of vision?

For many entrepreneurs, the allure of leadership lies in achieving scale, offering a sense of security and dominance. Scale undeniably brings advantages: efficiency, market influence, and competitive leverage. These outcomes are often lauded as progress and symbols of bold leadership. However, beneath the surface, the scale can carry hidden costs. Suppliers may struggle with shrinking margins, employees could face stagnant wages, and consumers might lose the benefit of choice. What is often hailed as growth can sometimes lead to monopolies that stifle innovation and harm the communities they claim to serve. These potential negative impacts of scale should prompt caution and critical reflection.

As organisations grow, their priorities naturally shift. Influence extends beyond markets and into policymaking, reshaping industries to favour the most prominent players.

While this evolution may seem logical from a competitive standpoint, it can sideline better ideas and restrict opportunities for smaller innovators. Are we measuring success by size alone, or are we holding growth accountable to a larger purpose? This tension highlights the need for strategic alignment and a broader perspective on success.

Visionary entrepreneurs differ from scale-driven followers. True visionaries view scale as a means, not an end. The growth holds value only when guided by purpose—when it uplifts employees, customers, shareholders, suppliers, and communities. This is the paradox: scale can amplify impact but risks becoming hollow without alignment to a meaningful vision.

Too often, leaders mistake scale for vision. The question is not whether growth is desirable—it usually is—but whether it elevates the organisation's mission and benefits all stakeholders. Without this alignment, growth becomes little more than a vanity metric—a pursuit impressive in size but lacking in purpose.

As a leader, have you ever wrestled with the tension between growth and purpose? How do you ensure your pursuit of scale reflects a vision that serves the greater good?

Reflection 3.12

SILENT BOARDROOMS

"It is not only what we do, but also what we do not do,
for which we are accountable."
– Molière (Stage name of Jean-Baptiste Poquelin,
Playwright and actor).

I once attended a board meeting on behalf of my travelling boss. While I had presented to boards before, this meeting revealed an unexpected side of corporate governance.

The setting was impressive: 16 board members with impeccable credentials, formal presentations prepared down to the last detail, and an unmistakable air of authority in the room. Yet, something felt amiss as each business unit presented its annual operating plan. Most board members seemed disengaged, focusing more on the snacks than the discussions. Only the Managing Director and the owner asked any probing questions.

I could not help but wonder: was this governance or merely a ceremony?

Here sat 16 brilliant individuals capable of offering diverse perspectives, yet their silence was deafening. The responsibility of oversight rested on just one or two voices. It felt paradoxical—a room designed for accountability yet lacking genuine engagement. Beneath the polished surface of protocols and formalities, an unsettling truth emerged: appearances often overshadow substance.

On a lighter note, I could not help but reflect: could higher sitting fees be inversely proportional to participation—

perhaps a new addition to Peter's Principles, where pay silences performance?

This experience lingered with me long after the meeting. It made me question how often we mistake structure for function. Are we more concerned with designing systems that look effective rather than ensuring they genuinely work? And why do we so readily accept these facades without challenging their purpose?

This issue extends beyond one boardroom. It is a challenge for all organisations: How do we ensure our governance processes are rooted in accountability and transparency? Perfect structures may offer a false sense of security, but without genuine accountability, they become little more than a convincing mirage.

Have you experienced a situation where meaningful participation was overshadowed by formality? How might proper accountability have shifted the outcome?

REFLECTION 3.13
MERIT – THE BOTTLED GENIE

"Is meritocracy so elusive, or are we afraid of what true merit might do to the status quo?"
– Author of this Book.

Is Merit the bottled genie of the corporate world? Tightly capped, it is brought out only when things go wrong—then pushed back in before it can shake things up too much. Time and again, I have seen this pattern. Companies spend generously hiring top talent, offering impressive titles and roles. Yet, once these bright minds step inside, they are often sidelined, their potential barely tapped. It raises the question: are we genuinely committed to meritocracy, or does true merit unsettle us because of its disruptive power?

Leadership is often at the heart of this dilemma. Entrepreneurs frequently see themselves as the all-knowing architects of their organisations, confident that their instincts surpass even the most qualified advice. Confidence is essential in leadership, yes, but unchecked hubris? That is something else entirely. When merit is stifled, the organisation loses more than opportunities for innovation and efficiency—it loses part of its soul.

But it is not just about ego. Even in talent-rich organisations, failures in governance and ethics are surprisingly common. Forensic audits often uncover glaring lapses—not because there were not smart people present, but because the system chose loyalty and conformity over independent thought. It is as if merit exists but remains muted, smothered under layers of control and mistrust.

Leadership in these situations tends to fall into two categories: those who stay silent to avoid upsetting the status quo and those who prioritise personal gain over organisational purpose. Both paths lead to the same outcome—an erosion of what could have been a vibrant culture of excellence. And the irony? By bottling up merit, these organisations risk losing precisely what they sought when they hired it: efficiency, quality, and transformation.

So, how do we let the genie out of the bottle? It is not enough to hire talented individuals and expect magic to happen. Actual change requires humility and courage at the top. Leaders must foster an environment where talent is empowered, not suppressed, and challenging norms are not perceived as a threat but as a catalyst for progress. Authentic leadership is not about controlling merit—it is about unleashing it to create lasting value and impact.

Have you witnessed merit sidelined in favour of conformity or loyalty? What would building a culture that genuinely values and unleashes talent take?

REFLECTION 3.14

THE COSTS OF MISSING ETHOS

"When the rich wage war, the poor die."
– Jean-Paul Sartre

The corporate world has its version of this: when leaders make decisions, employees, customers, and frontline workers often bear the brunt. The strategy may look brilliant in the boardroom, but the reality is usually starkly different.

I will never forget an incident where a quality issue arose in our product line. Customers demanded compensation, but my boss refused. His rationale? "We have a monopoly; we don't need to give in." In the short-term, this approach worked financially, and we avoided losses. But in the long run, trust was eroded. Customers began seeking alternatives, and internally, many of us questioned whether the values we preached meant anything.

This was not an isolated case. Failing to honour annual contracts is another frequent pattern, significantly when the economy slows or external crises arise. Leaders often rationalise such decisions as necessary, but the unseen costs—the erosion of trust, employee morale, and customer loyalty—can be immense.

The problem lies in a leadership mindset blinded by short-term wins. Decisions that ripple outward often fail to account for their human impact. The gap between strategy and humanity widens as the focus shifts from building trust to chasing numbers. Day-to-day choices—dismissing employee concerns, ignoring customer feedback, or prioritising cost-cutting over quality—gradually chip away at the leadership ethos.

But here is the truth: trust takes years to build and seconds to break. Leadership is not about perfection but about balancing results with ethical grounding. It is about recognising that decisions are not just about hitting targets—they are about people.

The next time we decide, we should pause and ask: Are we building something that will last? Or are we merely chasing short-term gains at the cost of long-term trust?

Have you witnessed leadership decisions prioritising gains over values? How could those decisions have been handled differently to preserve trust and ethos?

Reflection 3.15

TO BE OR NOT TO BE: A MANAGER'S DILEMMA

"In matters of style, swim with the current; in matters of principle,
stand like a rock."
– Thomas Jefferson.

Hamlet's existential question, "To be or not to be," echoes in the minds of corporate managers grappling with daily dilemmas. The tension between personal ethics and professional expectations often feels like an unresolvable tug-of-war. Managers make decisions that contradict their values—not because they want to, but because their systems demand it.

I have seen this play out firsthand. Some managers procrastinate on tough decisions, hoping the problem resolves itself. Others choose the path of least resistance, avoiding conflicts even when they know the cost. Then, some justify their actions with phrases like, "It's what's best for the company" or "I had no other choice." Yet, beneath these justifications lies a deeper discomfort: the realisation that their decisions might compromise something unknown or even painfully familiar to them.

The modern corporate world thrives on subjectivity cloaked as objectivity. What is celebrated as "value maximisation" often comes at the cost of fairness, empathy, and humanity. I have often heard one CEO demand "value extraction" in every action, turning efficiency into a mandate devoid of nuance or compassion.

Promotions, layoffs, and project approvals are rarely neutral decisions. A win for one side can feel like a loss for another, creating a paradox of perception. While these decisions may appear as strategic triumphs for the organisation, they can feel like personal betrayals for the individuals impacted, carrying a high emotional cost.

This paradox is not inherently wrong. When grounded in fairness and a genuine desire for balance, subjectivity can lead to thoughtful, ethical decisions. However, the pressures of quarterly targets, market competition, and internal politics often obscure that balance. Managers become reluctant enforcers of policies they may not fully believe in, trading long-term trust for short-term wins.

So where does that leave us? Corporate life will continue to present us with tough dilemmas. The real challenge is how we respond. Perhaps "to be or not to be" is less about choosing sides and more about finding the courage to make decisions that align with organisational goals and personal integrity. As Jefferson reminds us, in matters of principle, we must stand like a rock. It is not easy, but no one said leadership would be.

Have you ever made a decision at work that clashed with your values? Looking back, what would you have done differently?

REFLECTION 3.16

CXO HIRING – A GAME OF HIDE-AND-SEEK

"Transparency, honesty, and fairness are the pillars of trust, the foundation of any successful relationship—personal or professional."
– Unknown.

Recruiting CXOs should be about building trust and aligning visions, but in reality, it often feels more like a game of hide-and-seek. Employers and candidates alternate between the roles of hiders and seekers, driven by convenience and personal interests. This dynamic often breeds mistrust, and the consequences can be disastrous when it does.

Consider this case I encountered: A non-tech startup saw six CXOs exit in a single year. Alarm bells? Not for the promoters. They replaced each departing executive as quickly as they left, seemingly unfazed by the turnover. The cycle continued—new hires, quick exits—but the root cause was never addressed.

What went wrong? The promoters, seasoned entrepreneurs themselves, had perfected the role of the hider. Critical details—such as the true state of their innovation and the company's market readiness—were conveniently omitted during interviews. Yet, their expectations for the CXOs were sky-high: rapid valuations and immediate results despite the unspoken challenges.

Conversely, the CXOs, playing the seekers, failed to ask the right questions. Overconfidence closed their eyes to the glaring red flags—six exits in one year! They walked into their roles believing they could succeed where others had failed.

However, misplaced assumptions and misaligned priorities only added to the revolving door of exits.

This game of corporate hide-and-seek is far from harmless. When trust is compromised during recruitment, it cascades through the organisation. Distrust fosters disengagement, slowly eroding the very culture companies need to thrive.

The takeaway? Recruitment is not just about filling roles; it is about laying the groundwork for trust and collaboration. Employers must be honest about their challenges, and candidates must dig deeper, asking the right questions to uncover the complete picture. When both sides prioritise alignment over assumptions, the risk of this costly hide-and-seek game diminishes. This approach is not just beneficial—it is essential for successful CXO recruitment.

Have you seen instances where a lack of transparency during recruitment led to organisational trust issues? How can trust be rebuilt in such scenarios?

CLOSING NOTE: CRUCIBLE THAT MELTS AND TRANSFORMS

"Hard times refine us, not define us."
– Unknown.

When we dream of a fulfilling job and an ideal employer, we rarely imagine the corporate world as a jungle. Yet, it is precisely that—a dynamic, unpredictable terrain filled with surprises and challenges. It tests our ability to withstand its trials, pushing us to forge resilience, character, and clarity. We are tested and refined through competing priorities, ethical dilemmas, and shifting landscapes, emerging more assertively and self-aware.

In this intricate environment, peculiar realities surface: loyalty can become a double-edged sword, sycophancy can overshadow true merit, ambition can deviate from its intended purpose and chasing success can derail your character. They push us beyond into a crucible of self-discovery, revealing whether we will succumb, stumble, or transform. True transformation lies in outcomes, integrity, and resilience forged through the journey.

Beyond pursuing shareholder value, corporations are duty-bound to contribute positively to society. Through individual philanthropic efforts and corporate social responsibility, organisations and their leaders strive to align success with societal impact.

The following section delves into this responsibility, exploring the dynamics of corporate social responsibility, individual philanthropy, and the role of social entrepreneurship. At its core lies a critical question: why does "the missing impact" persist despite well-intentioned efforts? As we transition from the corporate world to the realm of philanthropy, you are invited to reflect on these complexities and chart a meaningful path toward a great society.

Part 4.0

PHILANTHROPY: FINDING THE SOUL

"Philanthropy is commendable, but it must not cause the philanthropist to overlook the circumstances of economic injustice which make philanthropy necessary."
– Martin Luther King Jr.

As we reflect on society's kaleidoscopic nature and the complexities of the corporate jungle, we realise that inequities perpetuate not only systemic flaws but also well-meaning but misaligned efforts. Society bears collective responsibility for these disparities, often exacerbated by corporate actions. In response, corporations, affluent individuals, and governments engage in philanthropic endeavours, yet their efforts frequently fall short, leaving an "impact gap."

Over the past six years, I have worked pro bono with ten enterprises in the livelihoods, preventive health, agri-producer companies, and skill development sectors. This experience has given me a front-row seat to the passion that drives this space and the struggles to translate that passion into enduring purpose.

This section invites philanthropy enthusiasts, entrepreneurs, and social leaders to examine the delicate balance between passion and measurable impact. It challenges us to question whether our well-intentioned actions create lasting change or contribute to optics. By exploring how philanthropy can align purpose with sustainable outcomes, we move closer to bridging the gap between giving and meaningful impact.

REFLECTION 4.1

CORPORATE CSR POWER: OUTCOMES OR OPTICS?

"If you want to lift yourself up, lift someone else."
– Booker T. Washington, African American Author.

Corporate Social Responsibility (CSR) is heralded as a game-changer—a tool with the potential to drive lasting social impact. But let's be honest—how often does it deliver on that promise? Too often, CSR feels like a performance designed more for optics than genuine outcomes.

Consider the reality. Companies host high-profile charity events, launch glossy reports, and launch flashy initiatives. Yet, how many of these efforts truly address deep-rooted social challenges? Nobel Laureate Milton Friedman once argued that a business's only responsibility is to increase profits. While perspectives on corporate responsibility have evolved, many CSR practices remain compliance-driven and focused on visibility rather than meaningful impact.

Take a simple example: Imagine corporations "ring-fenced" their immediate communities—perhaps a few thousand families around their operations. What if these businesses made long-term commitments to improve these neighbourhoods' education, healthcare, and livelihoods? The ripple effect could be transformative. Yet, such targeted, impactful approaches remain rare.

This issue is not exclusive to corporations. Social enterprises, despite their noble missions, face their own hurdles. Many lack the resources, sustainable business models, or entrepreneurial drive to survive in competitive markets. Meanwhile, some CSR funds are directed toward questionable purposes. Consider a corporate-backed initiative intended to support tribal artisans. Instead of empowering the artisans, most funds were spent on setting up a branded stall at an airport—great for corporate visibility, but what about the artisans?

The disconnect does not end there. Donors, too, often chase quick wins—projects that look good on paper but fail to create lasting impact. Nonprofits caught in this cycle may compromise their mission to meet donor expectations. It is a frustrating loop where passion collides with practicality and often loses.

What is the way forward?

The answer lies in shifting focus from optics to outcomes. Corporations must rethink CSR—not as a box to tick but as an opportunity to create lasting change. It is about money, collaboration, accountability, and long-term commitment.

Here is what that could look like:

- **Commit to Communities:** Focus on making measurable, sustained improvements in the lives of families around corporate operations.

- **Collaborate Meaningfully:** Corporates, nonprofits, and governments must break out of their silos and work around shared goals.

- **Measure Impact, Not Just Compliance:** Corporations and donors must hold themselves accountable for creating genuine, measurable change.

When done right, CSR is not just about looking good—it is about doing good.

Are corporations ready to measure their success by the depth of their impact rather than the height of their visibility?

REFLECTION 4.2

PURPOSE OR PRETENCE: WHEN IMPACT IS AN ILLUSION

"Generosity is giving more than you can, and pride is taking less than you need."
– Khalil Gibran.

A corporation recently invested nearly a crore in funding a tea stall at a high-visibility location. The plan seemed promising—on paper. But here is the twist: over three-quarters of the donation was allocated to capital expenses, raising questions about its necessity versus its impact. Sure, the project looked polished and impressive for optics. But how much of that money indeed reached the intended beneficiaries? Was this initiative about empowering communities or curating an image for the corporation?

Stories like these raise uncomfortable questions: Is this philanthropy or exploitation? Should governments allow such extravagances under the guise of CSR? When CSR funds prioritise corporate visibility at the expense of meaningful community impact, underserved populations become tools of pretence rather than beneficiaries of purpose.

The issue does not end with corporations. Nonprofits, too, face systemic pressures that can lead to compromises. To meet donor expectations, some organisations overstate their achievements or pivot their missions to align with funding trends—compromising their authenticity and long-term goals. Over time, these choices erode trust and shift focus away from creating tangible change.

The real challenge lies in redefining how we view accountability and success in philanthropy. For corporations, this means moving beyond symbolic gestures to engage directly with communities and understand their needs. It is about co-creating solutions and prioritising sustainable, long-term outcomes over momentary optics. For nonprofits, it means steadfast transparency and commitment to their mission, even under pressure to secure funding.

Authentic philanthropy is not about how much is spent but how wisely it is invested. Imagine CSR initiatives designed not to impress but to empower—where corporate resources fuel sustainable solutions and communities evolve from passive recipients to active participants in their growth. This vision requires courage and introspection from all stakeholders to shed pretence and embrace purpose.

The question is not whether philanthropy can drive change—it is whether we are ready to let it do so meaningfully.

How can corporations and nonprofits realign their efforts to ensure CSR funds create genuine, lasting impact rather than serving as tools of pretence?

REFLECTION 4.3

LEADERSHIP DYNAMICS IN THE SOCIAL SECTOR

"True leaders are like pebbles in a pond; their actions create ripples that drive change far beyond their initial intentions."
– Inspired by Tim Cook, Apple CEO.

Leadership in the social sector is a unique balancing act. While corporate leaders measure success through tangible metrics like profits and shareholder value, social leaders must pursue the more elusive goal of creating lasting impact—an intricate blend of progress, inclusion, and sustainability. This responsibility often brings contradictory pressures that require navigating a complex web of expectations.

Social leadership stories are often romanticised as heroic journeys fuelled by grit, purpose, and resilience. Yet, these qualities alone are not enough. Leadership in the social sector demands adaptability, humility, and the ability to reconcile the tensions between ideals and realities, donors and beneficiaries. For instance, the challenge of securing funding can push leaders to prioritise donor demands, even when they conflict with the actual needs of the communities they aim to serve.

A similar tension exists when nonprofits mentor social enterprises—ventures that aim to merge profit and purpose. While nonprofits often lead with passion and ideology, these qualities can unintentionally hinder progress. Social enterprises, which depend on practical strategies to thrive in competitive markets, sometimes find their growth stymied by a nonprofit mindset resistant to economic value creation.

The challenge deepens when leadership becomes performative—impressive on the surface but disconnected from real impact. True leaders do not merely articulate lofty ideals; they engage deeply with the complexities of their work, learning from both successes and failures. As Tim Cook wisely observed, leaders are like pebbles in a pond, creating ripples of transformation that extend far beyond their immediate reach.

Social impact does not happen in silos. Leaders must strike a delicate balance between ambition and practicality, passion and purpose. Unshackling themselves from rigid ideologies, they must focus on what truly works—not just what looks good. Leadership in the social sector is not about being a hero—it is about making a difference in grounded, impactful, and sustainable ways.

What strategies can social leaders adapt to bridge the gap between donor expectations and the authentic needs of the communities they serve?

REFLECTION 4.4

INCLUSIVE GROWTH: ILLUSION OR REALITY?

"Growth is never by chance; it is the result of forces working together."
– James Cash Penney, Founder of J.C. Penny.

Inclusive growth—it is a term often championed in boardrooms, promised by governments, and showcased in CSR reports. Yet, a closer look reveals a stark disconnect between aspirations and reality.

Over the years, India's economy has grown impressively—from \$1.7 trillion in 2010 to \$3.7 trillion in 2023. However, India's Human Development Index (HDI) rank fell from 119 in 2010 to 134 in 2023-24. While HDI values have seen marginal improvement, persistent inequality is glaring. If inclusive growth were genuinely happening, wouldn't this progress be reflected not only in GDP numbers but also in a significant uplift in the quality of life for all citizens?

The irony deepens when we examine corporate contributions. Industry and services sectors account for 84% of India's GDP (approximately \$3.1 trillion). Yet, Corporate Social Responsibility (CSR) spending for FY 2021-22 stood at ₹26,210 crore (\$3.2 billion)—a mere 0.08% of India's GDP in 2023. Numbers do not lie—this "fractional spend" barely addresses education, healthcare, and livelihood gaps.

Governments, too, have played their part—offering tax rebates, incentives, and protective policies to encourage corporate involvement in societal betterment. But the question remains: Are corporations doing enough? Imagine if every corporate entity adopted a "ring-fencing" strategy, committing to improving the quality of life for a few thousand families in their immediate surroundings, with HDI outcomes rivalling those of their promoters. Would this be such a radical idea?

Inclusive growth is not about rhetoric or glossy reports but tangible, measurable outcomes. It is about shared prosperity, ensuring corporate success translates into sustainable ecosystems where everyone has a fair shot at progress.

Are today's corporate strategies genuinely designed to drive inclusive growth, or are they merely token efforts skimming the surface of systemic inequalities?

REFLECTION 4.5

PROBLEMS ECLIPSE THE PASSION

"It is not enough to be compassionate. You must act."
– Dalai Lama.

India's staggering four million NGOs hold immense potential to drive social transformation. Yet, many are weighed down by internal challenges—credibility issues, funding constraints, and misaligned priorities. These pressing problems often eclipse the passion and purpose that fuel this sector.

Donors, wary of inefficiency and misuse, impose stricter controls, resulting in smaller grants and an overwhelming focus on compliance over outcomes. Ironically, corporations invest heavily in attracting top talent but hesitate to fund higher NGO administrative costs. This creates a paradox: expecting strategic impact from organisations operating on shoestring budgets.

A key barrier is a mistrust between donors and NGOs. Donors often view capacity-building as "overhead" and avoid investing in it, while NGOs, desperate for funding, overpromise and underdeliver. This vicious cycle stifles productivity, dilutes impact, and leaves systemic issues unresolved.

Imagine a world where passion converges with practical solutions, where NGOs are empowered to act as problem-solvers rather than just fund seekers. Transformation begins with donors and NGOs adopting a collaborative mindset, building trust, and working toward shared goals. To strengthen this partnership, NGOs must uphold transparency and accountability.

The paradox of problems eclipsing passion must be confronted head-on. Only then can the light of purpose outshine the shadows of inefficiency.

How can donors and NGOs realign their relationship to foster trust and drive meaningful, systemic change?

REFLECTION 4.6

VUCA CHALLENGE: THE SOCIAL SECTOR'S ACID TEST

"The greatest danger in times of turbulence is not the turbulence;
it is to act with yesterday's logic."
– Peter Drucker.

The VUCA (Volatile, Uncertain, Complex, Ambiguous) world demands resilience, adaptability, and systemic agility. The COVID-19 pandemic starkly exposed the vulnerabilities of the philanthropic ecosystem. Despite billions in funding, progress on critical metrics like the Human Development Index (HDI) remains alarmingly low.

Why isn't a rupee as efficient in the social sector as it is in business? While economic capital is vital, human capital, governance, and operational flexibility are equally critical—and often overlooked. NGOs frequently operate in rigid silos, struggling to adapt to external shocks, while donors prioritise short-term optics over long-term resilience.

Compounding the issue, some nonprofits and beneficiaries adopt an entitlement mindset, viewing philanthropy as a right rather than an opportunity. This dependency creates a fragile ecosystem ill-equipped to handle crises or drive sustainable progress.

The path ahead necessitates a shift in perspective. Philanthropy requires a fresh outlook that values outcomes, partnerships, and adaptability over isolated, transactional endeavours. Governments, corporations, and NGOs must unite as equals, leveraging their unique strengths to drive systemic change. Economic capital alone is insufficient; operational agility, strategic foresight, and a shared dedication to measurable impact are indispensable.

The question is, are we ready? In a VUCA world, survival and impact depend on embracing collaboration, fostering innovation, and building resilience. By reimagining how we work together, the social sector has the potential to transform intent into lasting impact, offering a hopeful vision for the future.

What mindset shifts and structural changes are essential for the social sector to thrive in a VUCA world and deliver measurable, systemic impact?

REFLECTION 4.7

DONOR FATIGUE: THE SILENT THREAT TO PHILANTHROPY

"The greatest danger in philanthropy is not lack of funds, but the erosion of trust between givers and doers."
– Unknown.

Donors give because they believe they can make a difference. But what happens when they stop believing? Donor fatigue is not just about an empty wallet but an empty sense of purpose. Imagine constantly giving but never seeing the impact. It is exhausting.

The truth is that donor fatigue creeps in when trust erodes. If you donate your time, money, or resources and all you receive are vague updates like "We're working on it" or flashy reports filled with colourful graphs but no clear outcomes, how long before you start asking, "Where is this going?" or "Why hasn't this made a real difference?"

This silent threat looms large over philanthropy. India's social sector attracts billions annually, yet the outcomes often feel underwhelming. Funds get entangled in inefficient processes, fragmented strategies, or initiatives that look good on the surface but fail to address real issues. Donors—individuals and corporates—grow weary when promises do not match tangible results.

Another challenge is the sheer scale of India's social sector—over four million NGOs, an overwhelming landscape for any donor to navigate. How do they sift through this ocean of organisations to find those truly making an impact? It is no surprise that many donors, faced with uncertainty and scepticism, disengage.

The post-COVID world has only exacerbated these issues. Budgets have tightened in sectors like BFSI, Energy, and IT—industries that are significant contributors to CSR in India. Donors now demand clear evidence that their money is making a difference. Vague updates and glossy brochures no longer suffice.

So, what is the way forward? Trust is the cornerstone of giving. NGOs must step up to demonstrate not just passion but precision. Donors need more than good intentions; they must see their contributions result in measurable, meaningful change. On the other hand, donors must move beyond transactional relationships. The most effective philanthropy arises from partnerships where donors and NGOs work together, aligning their efforts to maximise impact.

This collaborative approach is essential for reigniting trust and ensuring that philanthropy fulfils its potential as a force for good.

How can the social sector rebuild trust and ensure every contribution leads to tangible, lasting outcomes?

REFLECTION 4.8

IGNORED HIERARCHY OF NEEDS

"Philanthropy is not about money; it's about using whatever resources you have at your fingertips and applying them to improve the world."
– Melinda Gates.

Have you ever thought about what it takes to create lasting social change? It is not just about money. Funding is essential, but it is only one piece of a much larger puzzle—a hierarchy of needs often overlooked in the social sector.

Let's break it down:

Purpose → Money → Business Modelling → Networking → Mentoring.

The purpose is the foundation—it is why we do what we do. But without money, even the best intentions stall. Yet, it does not end there. Effective business models, strong networks, and thoughtful mentorships are essential to turning ideas into sustainable change. Unfortunately, these critical needs are often ignored or poorly addressed.

Consider **donor centrism.** Many donors believe writing a cheque is the ultimate way to help. It is not. While money solves some problems, the most profound impact often stems from expertise, guidance, and long-term collaboration. Then there's the flip side: some beneficiaries view philanthropy as a right, fostering an entitlement mindset that risks creating dependency rather than empowerment.

And what about civil societies? Too often, they become insular, failing to adapt to what beneficiaries or systems genuinely need. This disconnect leads to a frustrating cycle of inefficiency, where good intentions fail to translate into meaningful outcomes.

We must also challenge a damaging misconception: the idea that one must be rich, famous, or "successful enough" to give back. How often have we heard, "Once I have made it, I will contribute to society"? The truth is that genuine philanthropy does not wait for milestones. It begins wherever you are, with whatever you can offer.

Economic capital is vital, but it is not enough. Human capital, business acumen, strong management, and effective governance are equally crucial. Philanthropy that focuses solely on money is like a house built on sand—it might look impressive, but it won't last.

The way forward? It is not about individual efforts but collective action. Everyone in the ecosystem—donors, civil societies, and beneficiaries—must move beyond narrow priorities and align around a shared purpose. Only through collaboration can we address the overlooked hierarchy of needs and create a sustainable, meaningful impact.

How can the social sector address the overlooked hierarchy of needs to ensure transformative, lasting change?

REFLECTION 4.9

THE MISSING ELEMENT: PROFIT

"Profit is not a dirty word. It is what sustains the means to a greater end."
- Inspired by Muhammad Yunus.

In the social sector, "profit" often feels out of place—a term reserved for corporate boardrooms, not community centres or development initiatives. Yet, this discomfort with profit may be one of the most significant barriers to sustainable impact. Why is profit, or gain, seen as antithetical to purpose?

Passion has long been the cornerstone of social enterprises—a rallying cry for change and progress. But passion alone is not enough. Social enterprises risk becoming unsustainable without financial gain—whether through profit, efficiency, or measurable economic outcomes. This is not about turning charities into businesses; it is about recognising that financial viability is as critical to social impact as passion and purpose.

Consider this: Passion is powerful but can only take you far in a competitive market economy. Many social enterprises operate under severe disadvantages—limited resources, outdated business models, and inadequate governance. While their intent is noble, their inability to focus on financial sustainability often leads to failure, leaving beneficiaries worse off than before.

Here lies the irony: The passion that fuels these ventures often ignores the necessity of profit. Instead of empowering communities, this single-dimensional passion perpetuates dependence and inefficiency. True impact demands a multidimensional approach that aligns passion with profit to achieve the purpose.

Take the example of Aravind Eye Care System, a social enterprise that has mastered this equation. Founded in 1976 to eradicate needless blindness, Aravind combines compassion with operational excellence. While 60% of their patients receive free or heavily subsidised care, the organisation achieves financial sustainability by structuring its operations like a for-profit entity. Paying patients, who make up the remaining 40%, cross-subsidise the costs for those who cannot pay. Their streamlined processes and innovations in healthcare delivery allow them to treat millions of patients at a fraction of the cost of typical hospitals. Over four decades, Aravind has treated over 40 million patients and performed over 5 million surgeries while remaining financially viable.

Aravind's story shows that profit is not a dirty word; it is a driver of growth, innovation, and resilience. Just as passion fuels purpose, profit ensures its sustainability. Without it, even the most well-intentioned initiatives risk becoming short-lived, leaving behind unmet needs and unfulfilled promises.

The equation for success in the social sector is simple yet profound:

Passion + Profit = Purpose.

The true purpose is achieved when passion and profit align to create a lasting impact. The social sector must embrace this truth, shed outdated stigmas about profit, and recognise it as a vital component of meaningful change.

How can social enterprises and philanthropic efforts embrace the necessity of profit without compromising their purpose?

REFLECTION 4.10

THE PATH FROM TOKENISM TO TRANSFORMATION

"Accountability is the glue that ties commitment to results."
– Bob Proctor, Motivational speaker and self-help author.

Corporate Social Responsibility (CSR) programmes and social enterprises often set ambitious goals to drive societal change. Yet, many fall short, prioritising appearances over impact. What causes this disconnect, and how can it be resolved?

The CSR Conundrum: Symbolism Over Substance

For many corporations, CSR is more about visibility than meaningful change. High-profile charity events, glossy reports, and one-off initiatives dominate the narrative. But do these efforts address the deep-rooted problems they claim to tackle? Too often, the answer is no.

The issue lies in prioritising optics—a phenomenon I call "mandatory sympathising." Corporations allocate CSR budgets for maximum visibility but minimal long-term impact. Ironically, companies that excel in operational efficiency and innovation often abandon these principles when designing CSR strategies.

Many CSR initiatives unintentionally foster dependence rather than empowerment. A patronising attitude of "We are the givers, so we know best" often undermines real progress. Corporations must realise that creating a more equitable world also benefits their businesses. If CSR does not disrupt entrenched inequalities, what is the point?

Why Social Enterprises Struggle

Social enterprises, despite their noble missions, face steep challenges. They operate in markets dominated by resource-rich companies, often beginning with disadvantages such as:

- Limited scale and funding.

- Inefficient governance and outdated business models.

- A lack of urgency to adapt to market realities.

These internal challenges often outweigh the external competition. Worse, some ventures are set up to fail due to flawed strategies and poor execution. Financial institutions hesitate to lend to these unviable models, exacerbating the problem.

The Myth of Advocacy

Another challenge is that development lobbyists advocate policies and subsidies for social enterprises. While helpful, this does not address the fundamental inefficiencies within these ventures.

The proof? Some social enterprises thrive despite these challenges—their secret lies in addressing root causes and adopting sound practices. The takeaway is clear: internal fixes matter as much as external support.

So, What is Next?

The journey from tokenism to transformation requires urgency and decisive action:

1. **For Corporates:** CSR must transcend being a PR exercise and align with long-term societal goals. This means designing programmes that empower communities, address systemic inequities, and create measurable impact.

2. **For Social Enterprises,** Embrace financial sustainability, improve governance, and cultivate an entrepreneurial mindset. Focus on solving root causes instead of solely relying on external support.

With pressing social inequities growing more urgent by the day, CSR programmes and social enterprises must evolve beyond token gestures to deliver meaningful, systemic change. The window to transform good intentions into lasting impact is narrowing, and the time to act is now.

What steps can CSR initiatives and social enterprises take to move beyond symbolic efforts and create lasting, meaningful change?

REFLECTION 4.11

DUAL FORCE FOR TRANSFORMATIVE SOCIAL GOOD

"Capitalism has lifted millions out of poverty, but it must evolve to lift humanity to its highest potential."
- Inspired by John Mackey, Former CEO of Whole Foods Market,

Capitalism is a paradox—it creates immense wealth, drives innovation, and raises living standards. Yet, left unchecked, it can fuel inequality, exploitation, and environmental harm. The solution is not to dismantle capitalism but to transform it into a dual force for good: conscious capitalism and the cult of giving.

Conscious Capitalism: Profits with Purpose

Conscious capitalism challenges businesses to think beyond profits. Companies can drive progress by considering their impact on employees, communities, and the planet. Evidence shows businesses that embrace conscious capitalism often outperform peers by fostering trust, loyalty, and shared value with all stakeholders—not just shareholders.

The Cult of Giving: Generosity as a Norm

The cult of giving redefines generosity. It is not about enforced philanthropy or token charity acts. Instead, it envisions giving back as naturally as striving for success. This "cult" thrives on voluntary contributions and human willingness to make a difference, not external pressure or obligation.

The Transformative Power of Alignment

When conscious capitalism and the cult of giving come together, they create transformative outcomes. Ethical wealth creation meets purposeful giving, countering unchecked greed and systemic inequality to build sustainable, inclusive prosperity.

Science supports this alignment: Acts of generosity trigger dopamine release, fostering fulfilment. Giving benefits and uplifts the giver. Pairing this human inclination with conscious business strategies leads to enduring progress, not temporary fixes.

The Challenge

The challenge lies in authenticity. Giving without strategy risks ego-driven actions, and conscious capitalism without genuine commitment risks empty PR. True success demands integrity—rewriting systems, not redistributing resources.

Imagine a world where material success aligns with moral purpose, where achievement fuels collective well-being. This dual force—conscious capitalism and the cult of giving—can reshape our economic landscape to create inclusive, enduring prosperity.

The Call to Action

Inequality is not just a moral dilemma—it is a ticking social and economic bomb. Concentrated wealth leads to instability. By embracing this dual force, we can move from ambition for self to ambition for collective progress.

The time for transformation is now. We can chart a path toward a better future by uniting conscious capitalism and the cult of giving as a cohesive force. The world is watching—now is the time to act and lead.

How can you harness conscious capitalism and the cult of giving in your sphere of influence to create a meaningful, sustainable impact?

REFLECTION 4.12

THE PARADOX OF GIVING AS RECEIVING

"Only by giving are you able to receive more than you already have."
– Jim Rohn, Author and Motivational Speaker.

Philanthropy is often thought of as the act of giving—one person offering resources, time, or support to another. But over time, I have realised that giving is a misnomer. It is not just about the giver offering something to the receiver; the giver, in the process, receives something of equal or more superior value in return.

It might seem paradoxical: how can the giver receive when they are the one giving? The truth lies in this—giving is an act of service, and service offers more than just material goods. When we give, we also receive—the emotional satisfaction of making a difference, a sense of connection to others, or the purpose of contributing to something greater than ourselves.

For instance, when someone volunteers their time at a shelter or donates to a cause, they may give without expecting anything in return. Yet, what they receive is not always tangible. They experience gratitude, a sense of belonging to a cause, and the fulfilment of contributing to shared humanity. Giving does not diminish us; instead, it enriches us, fostering deeper connections and strengthening our sense of purpose.

This paradox of giving—where the giver also receives— was especially evident during the COVID-19 pandemic. Despite limited resources, people offered what they could:

time, care, and solidarity. In return, they found a profound sense of community empowerment and strengthened bonds through shared experiences.

By giving, we receive. This exchange is more than transactional; it is transformative. True philanthropy is not about one person elevating another—it is about shared experience and mutual growth, where both the giver and the receiver are enriched and inspired to continue their philanthropic journey.

How does the idea that "giving is a misnomer" change your understanding of philanthropy? How can you embrace the experience of giving as something that enriches you as well?

REFLECTION 4.13

COLLECTIVE CAPITALISM – A PHILANTHROPIC PATH FOR FARM SECTOR

"Alone, we can do so little; together, we can do so much."
– Helen Keller, American Author.

India's farm sector supports 800 million people—10% of the global population—yet remains in crisis. Despite contributing 16% to India's GDP, the industry is subsistence. Small landholdings, spiralling debts, and inefficient supply chains hinder progress. Traditional solutions like $50 billion in annual subsidies fail to deliver meaningful change.

Philanthropy must evolve from mere giving to empowerment, embracing Collective Capitalism—a model that unites collectivisation with entrepreneurial principles. This transformative approach can shift Indian agriculture from subsistence to sustainability.

The Promise of Collective Capitalism

At its core, Collective Capitalism leverages Farmer-Producer Organisations (FPOs) to combine smallholder strength with entrepreneurial efficiency. Imagine this: an investment of $200 billion over three years—just 15% of the annual philanthropic funds generated in the USA—could revolutionise Indian agriculture, doubling the agricultural GDP and uplifting 200 million farm families.

A Three-Pronged Strategy: Engage, Enhance, Ensure

1. **Engage Farmers Year-Round:**

   FPOs can create year-round opportunities through allied activities like poultry, dairy, and fisheries, ensuring consistent incomes and reducing migration.

2. **Enhance Productivity and Incomes:**

- Conduct land audits to optimise crop selection and practices.

- Build infrastructure for storage, processing, and value addition, reducing waste and boosting profits.

- Digitise supply chains for transparency and efficiency, helping farmers capture more incredible value.

3. **Ensure Economic Stability:**

- Facilitate predictable incomes via contract farming, hedging, and forward trading.

- Provide low-interest loans or performance-linked investments to maintain steady cash flows for FPOs.

The Role of Philanthropy and Corporates

For corporations and philanthropists, this is more than charity—it is an opportunity to drive large-scale change:

- **Corporate Engagement:** Invest in logistics, digitisation, and infrastructure, offering affordable services to FPOs.

Consumer goods companies can integrate FPOs into supply chains, creating stable income streams.

- **Philanthropic Leadership:** Supporting FPOs aligns with global goals like poverty alleviation and rural development, directly impacting 800 million lives.

- **Leadership Development:** Train local talent to manage FPOs, ensuring sustainability and innovation.

Challenges and the Path Forward

This vision faces challenges: Farmers must overcome mistrust and learn to work collectively. Corporates must balance profits with purpose. Policymakers must create an enabling environment that prioritises equity alongside market forces.

When farmers, corporations, philanthropists, and policymakers unite, Collective Capitalism can drive empowerment, dignity, and hope—turning subsistence into sustainability.

A Call to Action

India's agriculture sector stands at a crossroads. This is a once-in-a-generation opportunity to rewrite the future for 800 million people. Transitioning from subsistence to sustainability is not optional—it is imperative.

Empowering farmers is not just an economic necessity but a moral responsibility. This transformation demands collective will, strategic interventions, and a shared vision for progress. The time to act is now—for the prosperity of agriculture and the dignity of millions who depend on it.

How can Collective Capitalism be a transformative force for 800 million individuals reliant on agriculture, and what steps can philanthropists and corporations take to ensure it delivers dignity and sustainable economic progress?

REFLECTION 4.14

A FRAMEWORK TO MAKE THE DONOR'S DOLLAR WORK HARDER

"What gets measured gets improved."
– Peter Drucker.

When a dollar steps into the social sector—mainly for-profit social ventures—it often seems to lose its magic. Every dollar is expected to work hard in the corporate world, backed by a clear purpose, strategy, and measurable returns. Yet that same dollar frequently underperforms in the social sector, leaving many, especially those transitioning from corporate careers, puzzled.

Why does this happen? Social enterprises operate in harsh environments marked by unpredictable markets and limited resources. But businesses face challenges, too, so why does the dollar falter in a sector fuelled by passion and grit?

Of course, there are success stories—social ventures that make every dollar count. These outliers challenge us to rethink our approach, ask tough questions, and uncover what drives their success. What are they doing differently, and how can these practices guide the sector as a whole?

The performance of a donor's dollar matters as much in the social sector as in business—perhaps even more. Its productivity directly affects beneficiaries' lives, amplifying its social value. Social enterprises must treat donor funds not as charity but as investments demanding accountability, strategic thinking, and measurable outcomes. Over time, I have observed a framework that successful social enterprises share. It revolves around Five Elements and Three Dharmas, offering a robust blueprint for maximising impact.

The Five Elements: Building Blocks for Success

1. **Mission: The North Star**

   Social enterprises often struggle with an identity crisis between nonprofit ideals and for-profit pressures. A clear, compelling mission is vital—it must address an unmet need so significant that the organisation's absence would leave a vacuum. Without this focus, enterprises risk spreading themselves too thin and losing their way.

2. **Money: Beyond Donations**

   Some organisations thrive financially, while others barely survive. Why? Perspective matters. Treating donor funds as investments fosters financial discipline, more substantial budgeting, and better compliance—essential for long-term impact.

3. **Model: The Blueprint for Impact**

   A robust business model is not optional—it is essential. This includes clear strategies, sound governance, and adaptability. Donors need visibility into these models to ensure alignment with expectations. Success is not just about doing good—it is about sustainability.

4. **Markets: Assumptions vs. Reality**

   Just because you build it does not mean they will come. Many social entrepreneurs misjudge demand, assuming it will materialise without research. Products need unique value propositions to survive in competitive markets. As Jack Welch famously said, "Be paranoid about competition."

5. Manpower: The Core Strength

Passion brings people through the door, but fair pay keeps them there. Social enterprises must invest in their teams, offering fair compensation and opportunities for growth. The winning formula combines passion, fair pay, and quick wins to build trust in the mission and drive collective success.

The Three Leadership Dharmas: Non-Negotiable Principles

1. Cost Leadership

Every cost—direct or indirect—must be accounted for. Social enterprises must embed cost advantages into their systems to stay afloat and protect beneficiaries from external shocks.

2. Productivity Leadership

Social ventures often face challenges involving economies of scale. Optimising resource use and increasing operating efficiency can offset these disadvantages, ensuring that every resource contributes fully.

3. Price Leadership

Operating in low-margin spaces, social enterprises often provide minimally value-added products. The key to premium pricing lies in delivering quality, maintaining integrity, and reducing intermediaries to maximise value.

The Takeaway

The dollar's underperformance in the social space is not inevitable. With the right mindset and frameworks, social entrepreneurs can maximise their impact and foster optimism and motivation. Accountability, strategic thinking, and disciplined execution must become the cornerstones of every social venture.

Indian Vedantic thought reminds us that **life is a journey from the unseen to the seen and back again to the unseen.** In this fleeting "seen" phase, social enterprises must strive to manifest their potential magnificently. Their bottom line is not just about organisational metrics; it is about transforming lives. Every dollar—and every effort—counts in this mission.

Which of these Five Elements or Three Dharmas resonates most with your experience?

REFLECTION 4.15

MINDSET SHIFT – THE SUCCESS IMPERATIVE

"You cannot solve a problem with the same mindset that created it."
– Albert Einstein.

The Purpose paradox often comes alive when nonprofits aim to transition into for-profit social enterprises. Economic empowerment, the crux of social transformation, demands this shift. But here is the challenge: how do you balance purpose with profit without compromising your mission?

This tension became stark during the COVID-19 pandemic's "Lives vs. Livelihoods" debate. While saving lives took precedence, livelihoods bore the brunt. Billion-dollar stimulus packages offered temporary relief, but sustaining long-term employment required more. With their community ties, nonprofits seemed poised to step in. Yet, the leap from project-driven philanthropy to sustainable enterprise proved daunting.

Where Nonprofits Struggle

Nonprofits traditionally operate with a "project mindset"—tasks are defined by donor priorities and measured against short-term objectives. However, transitioning to a for-profit social enterprise shifts the focus to sustainability, scalability, and maximum impact. It is like moving from navigating a well-marked trail to exploring an open field. This shift demands more than resources; it requires a fundamental change in mindset.

Two Key Shifts for the Transition

1. The Ownership Mindset

Transitioning to a for-profit model means owning the mission and every decision—across mission, Money, Model, Markets, and Manpower. Unlike donor-driven priorities, leaders must define their vision, take accountability, and ensure alignment with measurable goals.

Ownership is not about control; it is about deep accountability. Every rupee spent must have a clear, long-term purpose. In a for-profit world, unpredictability is the norm, and success depends on agility—pivoting, adapting, and swiftly making tough calls.

2. Risk Appetite

Risk is unavoidable in for-profits, but many nonprofits treat it as the donor's burden. For-profit ventures demand a new approach:

- Anticipate and prepare for risks proactively.
- Treat risks as opportunities for growth and innovation.
- Balance planning with the courage to embrace uncertainties.

The rewards of risk-taking often outweigh the potential downsides. Without embracing risk, scaling impact and innovation becomes impossible.

Let's Talk About Profit

Many nonprofits face a mindset block: "Profit and Passion don't mix." This could not be farther from the truth. Profit is not the enemy; it is a tool for sustainability and growth.

When used responsibly, profit amplifies purpose. It fuels scalability, solves significant problems, and creates enduring change. Without it, nonprofits risk stagnation when donor funding dries up. Profit becomes problematic only when it is pursued as an end in itself.

So, What is Next?

The COVID era exposed deep economic inequalities that governments alone cannot resolve. Nonprofits have an unparalleled opportunity to step up, requiring an "economic growth mindset." Moving beyond survival means building scalable, impactful social enterprises that merge purpose with profit. The time to act is now—embracing this mindset is no longer optional; it is imperative for lasting impact.

What specific mindset or operational shift can your organisation make today to transition from short-term projects to a sustainable, long-term impact model?

CLOSING NOTE: PHILANTHROPY: PURPOSE OVER POMP

"No one has ever become poor by giving."
– Anne Frank (1929–1945): A Voice of Resilience, Hope, and Humanity.

My reflections on philanthropy may have stirred a mix of emotions and opinions. If progress towards India's SDG goals remains insignificant despite years of effort, we must ask ourselves: where are we going wrong? Is it a lack of resources or perhaps a misalignment of intentions?

We witness immense generosity and a burning passion to make a difference, yet the impact often feels fragmented and fleeting. Glossy CSR initiatives grab headlines while grassroots NGOs struggle to balance noble missions with limited resources. Even well-intentioned donors grapple with the efficacy of their contributions.

This raises a critical question: how do we transcend passion and create philanthropy that transforms lives? True impact demands more than writing cheques or launching high-profile programmes. It necessitates a deep understanding of ground realities, a commitment to long-term collaboration, and unwavering trust.

At its core, philanthropy is about recognising our shared humanity. It is a reciprocal act in which every contribution, no matter how small, enriches both the giver and receiver. In those moments of genuine connection and shared purpose, we uncover the true soul of philanthropy—a force capable of uplifting not just individuals but our entire society.

But good intentions alone are not enough. To translate purpose into progress, we must reimagine philanthropy and reorient ourselves toward transformational impact. This requires leadership in the corporate and social sectors that unite stakeholders, inspire action, and drive transformation. Leaders are the compass that guides decisions, fosters collaboration, and navigates the complexities of social change.

What is leadership, and what are its dimensions? The next part of the "Leadership Prism: Refract Power" series will explore leadership's potential to drive transformation, foster resilience, and shape a better future. Leadership is not just about individual capability—it is the engine that propels collective progress and amplifies the power of purpose.

Part 5.0

LEADERSHIP PRISM: REFRACT THE POWER

"Leadership is not about being in charge. It is about caring for those in your charge."
– Simon Sinek, Leadership Coach and Speaker.

In today's kaleidoscopic society, where patterns and perspectives shift rapidly, many find themselves adrift in the corporate jungle. Leadership must transcend the narrow confines of performance metrics and reimagine its purpose. It is neither a title nor the mere accumulation of power; leadership is about service, vision, and the responsibility to inspire.

If leadership were a prism, it would refract power with precision, transforming it into a lasting impact. True leadership focuses and amplifies light—illuminating paths for others, inspiring collective progress, and fostering a legacy of meaningful change.

This section examines the delicate balance leaders must maintain to embody this vision. Through stories of triumph and failure, it challenges conventional wisdom and highlights the profound difference between holding authority and wielding it with intention and care.

Leadership is a paradox: a fusion of strength and vulnerability, decisiveness and empathy, vision and adaptability. How can leaders embrace these contrasts and transform power into purposeful action?

REFLECTION 5.1

LEADERS: BORN, MADE, OR CHOSEN?

"Leaders aren't born; they are made. And they are made just like anything else, through hard work."
– Vince Lombardi, Legendary American Football coach.

Are leaders born, or are they made? This question has sparked debates in boardrooms, classrooms, and over coffee tables for years. The truth, as always, lies somewhere in the middle. Leadership in the corporate world does not seem to be purely an inborn gift or a skill you can fully master through training. Instead, it develops as a response to life—shaped by experiences, external challenges, and the moment's demands.

For many, leadership becomes little more than a job title or a list of responsibilities. Driven by external pressures like market demands or competition, leadership styles often swing from too controlling to overly accommodating. However, these shifts are usually superficial and lack genuine intent. What looks like kindness in good times can vanish when the going gets tough.

Ironically, success can also distort leadership. While it is worth celebrating, it sometimes inflates egos. Some leaders become more focused on protecting their power than driving real progress. They surround themselves with people who agree with them, shutting out dissent and fresh ideas—not because these lack value but because they challenge the comfort of the status quo.

This shallow version of leadership works when times are good. Reactive or insecure leaders often thrive when conditions are favourable. But when things fall apart, they quickly blame external factors and fail to take responsibility for the fallout.

True leadership is something else entirely. It is not about titles or authority—it is about choosing to make a lasting impact. Like a prism breaking light into a spectrum, real leadership takes raw power and turns it into something meaningful. This requires self-awareness, a commitment to strong values, and the courage to face challenges with clarity and resolve.

This is a chance to reflect on our leadership. It is not about whether we were born with or learned it—it is about what we choose to do with it. Every day, we decide whether to use our influence to create lasting change or simply react to what is happening around us.

So, what about you? Are you using your leadership to bring purpose and impact, or are you just responding to pressures? What steps can you take to turn your influence into something that lasts beyond the moment?

REFLECTION 5.2

THE LEADERSHIP TRINITY – PURPOSE, PASSION, AND PROFIT

"The best leaders are not those who seek power or profit for its own sake but those who harness their passion and purpose to inspire others and create meaningful impact."
– John C. Maxwell, Leadership Coach.

Leadership today is about more than climbing the corporate ladder or hitting quarterly targets. It is about balancing deeper goals that connect careers, societal impact, and personal growth. These aspects of life no longer stand apart—they are like tributaries flowing into the same river. The challenge for leaders is to navigate these interconnected demands while staying true to themselves.

I call this the modern leadership paradox: balancing creating wealth, maintaining personal freedom, driving growth in uncertain times, and staying rooted in core values. While it is not easy, these challenges also bring an opportunity to redefine leadership as a blend of purpose, passion, and profit.

I think of this as a kind of **"modern-day spirituality."** It is not about rituals or abstract ideals but about aligning your passions with a meaningful purpose and driving impactful and profitable ventures. These are not opposing forces—they are partners. Profit is not the enemy of purpose; it is the energy that helps you turn big ideas into reality and scale your impact.

True leadership happens at the crossroads of passion, purpose, and profit. Passion gives us the energy to move forward, purpose provides direction, and profit gives us the means to act. Together, they create a foundation for a legacy that goes beyond personal success to shape businesses, communities, and the lives of others. What matters most is not just what we achieve but the lasting impact we leave behind.

Take a moment to reflect: Are your leadership choices guided by passion, grounded in purpose, and supported by profit? What steps can you take to unite these elements and build a legacy that truly matters?

REFLECTION 5.3

THE COURAGE OF VULNERABILITY

"A leader knows the way, goes the way, and shows the way—often by being open, honest, and vulnerable."
- John C. Maxwell.

Vulnerability.   For many of us, it is a word that feels uneasy—like stepping into a room and laying down your armour in front of critics. But what if I told you that vulnerability isn't a weakness? It is one of the most profound strengths a leader can have.

When you admit you don't have all the answers, does it make you less of a leader—or more relatable? When you share your struggles, does it diminish your authority—or inspire greater trust? Vulnerability is not about perfection; it is about connection. It shows your team that you're human in this together and that it is okay to take risks, fail, and rise again.

Myths vs. Realities of Vulnerability:

- **Myth**: Vulnerability means being weak.

  Reality: It is an act of courage and the foundation for trust.

- **Myth:** Vulnerability is about oversharing.

  Reality: It is about sharing the right things at the right time to inspire and empower.

- **Myth**: Vulnerability is unprofessional.

  Reality: True professionalism thrives on transparency, authenticity, and accountability.

Yes, being vulnerable can feel scary. You might fear judgement or even rejection. But isn't that true for most things worth doing? The reward far outweighs the risk—stronger relationships, a more engaged team, and a culture of trust where people feel safe to innovate and grow.

So here is the question: Are you willing to let your guard down? To show the person behind the title? That is where authentic leadership begins—when we embrace the courage of vulnerability.

What is stopping you from embracing vulnerability as a leader? How did it impact your relationships or team dynamics if you've tried it before? What is one small step you can take to begin if you have not?

REFLECTION 5.4

THE ART OF LEADERSHIP BALANCE

"Leadership is not about making the right choice every time but about harmonising the demands of the present with the vision for the future."
– Anonymous.

In the corporate world, leadership often feels like walking a tightrope—balancing today's immediate needs with tomorrow's long-term aspirations. Leaders perpetually face competing priorities: meeting quarterly targets, responding to market pressures, or maintaining stakeholder confidence, all while striving to build a sustainable, visionary path forward.

Short-term decisions can deliver quick wins, such as stabilising finances or boosting morale, but they can also risk draining resources or stifling innovation. Conversely, pursuing long-term strategies—like investing in disruptive technologies or entering uncharted markets—requires sacrifices in the present, such as tighter budgets or delayed profitability. The real challenge lies in finding a way to reconcile these seemingly opposing demands.

Take, for instance, the decision to invest in a transformative technology platform. The long-term potential—enhanced efficiency, scalability, and competitive advantage—is evident. Yet, the immediate costs, risks, and resistance from stakeholders can feel overwhelming. Managing such decisions takes vision, courage, and finesse, ensuring that short-term compromises do not derail the broader mission.

What does it take to achieve this balance successfully? Strategic foresight to anticipate the ripple effects of decisions. Humility to accept that not every outcome will be perfect. Adaptability to adjust course when reality diverges from expectations. Above all, clarity of vision ensures that short-term actions align with long-term values and aspirations.

True leadership does not choose between short-term gains and long-term goals—it finds a way to serve both. It creates value today while building the foundation for tomorrow.

How do you ensure your leadership decisions balance immediate demands with long-term vision? Are your actions today aligned with your organisation's future values and aspirations?

REFLECTION 5.5

NO EXCEPTIONS: EVEN THE BOSS NEEDS A BOOST

"Appreciation can make a day—even change a life. Your willingness to put it into words is all that is necessary."
– Margaret Cousins, the First woman magistrate in India and co-founded the All India Women's Conference (AIWC) in 1927,

Most self-help courses focus on self-motivation, and while it is vital, they often overlook a simple truth: no one is entirely self-sufficient. Even the most driven individuals occasionally need external encouragement. This applies to bosses, too—a reality we rarely acknowledge.

A senior leader once said, "I need motivation, too." At first, this statement seemed surprising. Why would someone who exudes confidence and control need motivation from their team? But the truth is that leadership can be isolating. The higher you climb, the fewer opportunities you have for genuine appreciation or constructive feedback.

This concept is often misunderstood. Many assume that "motivating the boss" means empty flattery or pandering, but it is far more meaningful than that. The true motivation for leaders comes from acknowledging their efforts, offering sincere feedback, and showing that their work makes a difference. It is about fostering mutual respect and creating an environment where even leaders feel valued and inspired.

Like anyone else, leaders draw energy from those around them. A heartfelt thank you, recognition of tough decisions, or proactive problem-solving can make a significant difference. Motivating your boss is not about "managing up"—it is about recognising that leadership is a shared journey where inspiration flows both ways.

Next time you interact with your bosses, ask yourself: Are you contributing to their motivation as they guide yours? Leadership is not a one way relationship; it thrives on mutual encouragement and shared accountability.

Do you actively take opportunities to motivate those who led you, or do you assume they are immune to the need for encouragement?

REFLECTION 5.6

PASSIVE LEADERSHIP – POTENTIAL CURSE?

*"Inaction breeds doubt and fear. Action breeds
confidence and courage."*
– Dale Carnegie.

The development sector often adheres to a unique set of ideals. Leaders are encouraged to embody empathy, prioritise stakeholders, and measure success using intangible, qualitative metrics. While these values are well-meaning, they sometimes foster passivity rather than action.

Consider this notion: "Thou shalt measure success not by the end but by the means." It sounds noble—emphasising the process over the outcome. But what happens when this philosophy sidelines the very people we aim to serve? Can passivism drive transformative change when the ultimate goal is improving lives?

Then there's the rallying cry: "Development work is riddled with challenges." While it is true that this field is challenging, such statements often reinforce stereotypes that success is nearly impossible. The frequently quoted statistic—"90% of social enterprises fail just like startups"— raises a more profound question: Should failure ever be the accepted norm when the stakes involve the most vulnerable communities?

We also cannot ignore the trust deficit in donor relationships. Nonprofits often produce exhaustive proposals, audits, and reports to prove their credibility. Why must organisations jump through such hoops to justify their existence? If donors do not trust them, why partner with them in the first place?

This reflection is not about discrediting development leaders or their work. Many carry extraordinary passion and vision. But it is a call to action to question stereotypes and challenge passive approaches:

- Are we hiding behind ideals like empathy and resilience instead of embracing proactive, accountable leadership?

- Are we normalising failure in a sector where success is a matter of life and death?

Leaders in any sector cannot afford to be passive. In development, where the stakes often involve poverty, hunger, and inequality, the cost of inaction or misplaced priorities is too high. Passive leadership is not just a missed opportunity—it is a betrayal of the mission to serve and create lasting change.

How can development leaders break free from leadership stereotypes to create meaningful, measurable change?

REFLECTION 5.7

TRANSACTIONAL LEADERSHIP – CRISIS RESPONSE OR THE NEW NORMAL?

"The ultimate measure of a leader is not where they stand in moments of comfort and convenience, but where they stand at times of challenge and controversy."
– Martin Luther King Jr.

Adolf Hitler's chilling words—"If you win, you need not explain. If you lose, you should not be there to explain"—starkly reflects a mindset that, while extreme, resonates in specific modern workplaces. Transactional leadership thrives in crises, focusing on short-term survival and measurable outcomes. But has it quietly become the new normal?

The COVID-19 pandemic sharpened the focus on this question. Leaders faced extraordinary pressure: livelihoods were on the line, markets were volatile, and decisions required speed. This often meant reverting to cutthroat measures—layoffs, cost-cutting, and relentless performance demands. Metrics usually overshadowed morale, making transactional leadership the default approach.

Here is the issue: When leadership becomes purely transactional, it sacrifices long-term trust and loyalty. Employees become resources to manage rather than people to nurture. While this may achieve short-term goals, it risks leaving behind a disengaged workforce, fractured relationships, and a culture prioritising results over resilience.

During this period, the contrast between transactional and transformational leaders became striking. Transactional leaders approached crises as survival battles, focusing on immediate wins at any cost. In contrast, transformational leaders saw crises as opportunities to lead with empathy and care. They balanced tough decisions with compassion, recognising that leadership is not just about what you achieve but how you achieve it.

Compassion is not a luxury, especially in times of crisis—it is a necessity. It builds trust, inspires loyalty, and lays the groundwork for long-term success. Ignoring compassion leads to cultures of fear and alienation, where employees disengage instead of rallying together.

So, is transactional leadership simply a crisis response, or has it become the new normal? The answer depends on our choices. Leadership is not about avoiding tough decisions—it is about making them with humanity and foresight. Crises will come and go, but how we lead through them defines the legacy we leave behind.

In moments of crisis, have you observed a shift toward transactional leadership? What impact did it have on morale, trust, and long-term culture?

REFLECTION 5.8

ARROGANCE: A BYPRODUCT OF SUCCESS?

"Nearly all men can stand adversity, but if you want to test a man's character, give him power."
- Abraham Lincoln.

Aggression, arrogance, and an unrelenting focus on domination—traits once frowned upon—seem to define the corporate playbook for success in some quarters. In the race to outpace the competition and achieve monumental results, confident leaders adopt a machismo-driven leadership style, relishing their power and achievements. However, what starts as inspiring leadership often transforms into authoritarianism, where success becomes oppressive for those working under them.

I have observed firsthand how some leaders, emboldened by their achievements, become unrecognisable. Their focus shifts from inspiring teams to driving them mercilessly. Collaboration turns into coercion, and ambition morphs into exploitation. Employees, once valued contributors, start feeling like mere cogs in a machine. Over time, this behaviour does not just erode morale—it stifles creativity, breeds resentment, and drives talent away.

Why does this happen? Success often creates a bubble of invincibility around leaders, particularly when it comes quickly or at scale. They begin to equate their position with absolute authority, mistaking short-term victories for long-term mastery. The arrogance born of unchecked success closes their eyes to the very people who helped achieve their triumphs. Employees, feeling overworked and undervalued, sometimes brand such leaders as **"slave drivers."** This harsh label reflects a reality where the focus shifts to results over relationships, outputs over individuals, and pressure replaces motivation.

The ripple effects of this aggressive style extend far beyond the immediate team. Organisational culture suffers, trust diminishes, loyalty wanes, and a fear-driven environment emerges. In such workplaces, openness takes a back seat to survival, undermining employee well-being and the organisation's long-term sustainability.

Leadership requires humility to stay grounded and empathy to motivate teams. Success should be a platform for empowerment, not an excuse for arrogance.

Have you ever noticed how success has changed your behaviour or that of someone you worked with? How did it affect the team or workplace, and what could have been done differently to ensure humility and empathy were not lost?

REFLECTION 5.9

ALEXANDERS: PRODUCTS OF A COMPETITIVE SOCIETY

"Power doesn't corrupt people; people corrupt power."
– William Gaddis, American Novelist.

History remembers Alexander the Great as a conqueror who reshaped the world through domination. Today, we see many modern "Alexanders" around us—people who use their wealth, influence, or fear to control their environments. They exist in corporations, politics, communities, and even within families. Their methods might have changed over time, but their goal is the same: to dominate, whether it is markets, minds, or lives.

Here is the twist: these Alexanders did not appear out of nowhere. They are products of the systems and societies that reward aggression and idolise success at all costs. We celebrate those who rise to the top, even if it means sacrificing fairness and collaboration to get there. These leaders do not compete with others—they exploit the systems that enabled their rise, finding ways to strengthen their grip through any vulnerabilities they can manipulate.

This is not just theory—it is everywhere. Think of monopolistic corporations that crush smaller players or politicians who manipulate public opinion to silence opposition. The media sometimes amplifies the powerful's voices while ignoring those less privileged. This creates a world where power seems to overshadow shared progress, and the result is often a loss of dignity, freedom, and trust.

What is worse is how often we, as a society, allow this to happen. We normalise behaviours that harm the collective good by admiring dominance and ignoring exploitation. In doing so, we make progress at the cost of humanity—leaving behind those who need help the most.

So, how do we change this? It starts with recognising the patterns around us. Power does not mean control; leadership does not have to be about conquest. Instead of admiring aggression, we can value collaboration, equity, and mutual respect. We must also consider what we reward in leaders and what behaviours we encourage in our communities and workplaces.

Have you ever noticed signs of this domination culture in your life or workplace? What small steps could you take to challenge it or help shift the focus toward fairness and shared growth?

REFLECTION 5.10

THE LEADERSHIP MIRROR: WHEN CRISIS REVEALS CHARACTER

"Man is nothing but what he makes of himself."
– Jean-Paul Sartre.

Have you ever noticed how a leader's true character comes to light not during moments of success but in times of crisis? It is fascinating, isn't it? The same challenging situation can bring out the best in some leaders while exposing the cracks in others. Adversity acts like a mirror—it strips away pretences and shows what is beneath the surface.

I saw this firsthand during a major organisational crisis. Two leaders faced the same storm—a significant market downturn. One, focused on protecting his image, crafted elaborate presentations to justify poor performance and shift blame. The other took an entirely different route. She gathered her team, acknowledged the reality of the situation, and openly admitted she did not have all the answers. She then brainstormed solutions, leaning into the team's shared values and collective strength.

The results could not have been more different. The first leader's team disengaged, with key members jumping ship when they were needed most. Though still battling challenges, the second leader's team became more cohesive, innovative, and motivated in tackling their problems. The difference? Character.

Character-driven leadership is not about playing it safe or projecting strength. It is about living your values, especially in tough times. When leaders focus on appearing perfect, they create a culture where everyone feels pressured to do the same. But when leaders show up as their authentic selves—vulnerabilities and all—they create a reassuring space for trust, connection, and real growth.

The truth is, leadership character is not fixed. It is dynamic. It evolves through how we choose to act in moments of difficulty, how we treat others when no one's watching, and how we reconcile our ideals with our actions. The mirror of leadership does not just show us who we are—it reveals who we are becoming, inspiring us to strive for better versions of ourselves.

Leadership driven by character is about alignment. It is not about perfection but ensuring that our actions reflect our values. When what we do in private matches what we stand for in public, we build trust that carries teams and organisations through any storm. Authenticity inspires, not because it is flawless, but because it is real, empowering us to take control of our leadership journey.

Think about a challenging situation you've faced as a leader. How did your actions reflect your true character at that moment? What did that experience reveal about the leader you are—and the one you aspire to become?

REFLECTION 5.11

THE PRICE AND PRIZE OF AUTHENTIC LEADERSHIP

"The privilege of a lifetime is to become who you truly are."
– Carl Jung.

As leaders, we often wear masks to hide our flaws, projecting strength and competence. But true strength lies in acknowledging and accepting our imperfections. This idea forms the essence of authentic leadership, yet it is not always straightforward. Leaders constantly balance maintaining their core values with evolving to meet new challenges. The real question is: How do we grow without losing sight of who we are?

I have seen this tension play out in countless boardrooms and meetings. Leaders often feel the pressure to project confidence, appearing to have all the answers. They wear the "leadership mask"—a carefully curated image of unshakeable competence. However, as Professor Herminia Ibarra explains, this is not inherently bad. The **authenticity paradox** suggests that adapting your leadership style to meet the role's demands is essential for growth. The challenge lies in evolving while staying true to your values.

I experienced this firsthand during a career shift from a line to a staff role in business transformation. The temptation to cling to my old leadership style was intense—it had worked for me before. Yet, authenticity is not about remaining static; it is about evolving purposefully. It is not about resisting change but about aligning who you're becoming with the values that define you.

Here is the takeaway: Authentic leadership does not mean discarding the mask entirely or rigidly sticking to one way of leading. Instead, it is about understanding when to adapt your style to meet new demands while staying anchored to your core values. The paradox is that authenticity is not about "being yourself" in the most rigid sense—it is about growing into your aspirational self.

Yes, authentic leadership has a cost—it requires vulnerability, self-awareness, and the courage to evolve in full view of others. But the reward is profound: deeper trust, stronger relationships, and a legacy built not on a title but on genuine alignment between who you are and how you lead.

When have you had to adapt your leadership style to meet the demands of a new challenge or role? How did you navigate the tension between staying true to your values and evolving as a leader? What did you learn about authentic growth?

REFLECTION 5.12

EMPATHY: THE EMOTIONAL GLUE OF LEADERSHIP

"Empathy is about finding echoes of another person in yourself."
– Mohsin Hamid, Pakistani-British Novelist.

Leadership often emphasises vision, strategy, and results, but empathy acts as the emotional glue, holding teams together and fostering genuine connections. While vulnerability allows leaders to show up authentically, empathy bridges the gap between individuals, creating bonds that build trust, loyalty, and collaboration.

I recall a colleague who returned to work after a personal crisis, struggling to regain focus. Her manager could have dismissed her concerns or offered generic advice, but instead, he simply asked, "How can I support you?" That simple question meant more than any solution could. It was not about fixing the problem but being present, understanding, and offering support.

Empathy in leadership is not about solving every issue or taking on everyone's burdens. It is about listening, recognising unspoken struggles, and showing genuine care. Leaders often feel they must project authority and provide answers. Yet, the most profound leadership moments come from simply being there for others, offering a listening ear rather than directives.

Empathy is sometimes dismissed as a "soft skill," secondary to results and efficiency in fast-paced environments. But this could not be further from the truth. Empathy builds trust, inspires loyalty, and strengthens relationships. Empathetic teams are more engaged, creative, and resilient. They do not just follow instructions—they commit wholeheartedly because they feel understood and valued.

Empathy, however, requires balance. It is not about being endlessly available or sacrificing boundaries. It is about creating moments of connection that show people they matter. When leaders lead with empathy, they do not just manage teams—they transform them into communities where collaboration thrives, challenges are tackled with a shared purpose, and trust becomes the foundation for success.

True leadership is not about standing apart from your team but standing with them. Empathy is the glue that binds individuals together, turning goals into shared missions and workplaces into communities.

Reflect on a time when you led with empathy. How did it affect your team or the individuals involved? What steps can you take to ensure empathy remains a cornerstone of your leadership approach?

REFLECTION 5.13

THE POWER OF EMOTIONS IN LEADERSHIP

"Water adapts without losing its essence, flowing into spaces that need it most. The best leaders are like water."
– Lao Tzu.

Have you ever walked into a room and felt the tension before anyone said a word? Emotions are always present, even when they are not expressed out loud. As leaders, it is easy to dismiss them as distractions and focus solely on the task at hand. However, emotions are woven into the fabric of team dynamics. They reveal the underlying currents, and when understood, they can transform challenges into opportunities.

I remember a situation where two highly skilled team members were constantly at odds. Their tension was not just a personal issue—it was affecting the entire team. It would have been easy to step in, enforce some rules, and move on. Instead, I decided to listen. What I uncovered had little to do with the work itself. Both felt overlooked and undervalued. We addressed the real issue by creating a space where they could voice their feelings. To my surprise, what started as conflict evolved into collaboration.

That experience taught me something important: emotions are not roadblocks—they are signals. They can lead you to solutions that would otherwise remain hidden when approached with curiosity instead of avoidance.

Leadership is not about ignoring emotions or letting them take over. It is about recognising when they are at play and responding thoughtfully. Leaders who understand the emotional undercurrents and respond with care build teams where:

- Conflicts become opportunities for growth
- Trust becomes the foundation of every interaction
- Fear gives way to creativity and innovation

Emotional intelligence does not mean being overly accommodating or avoiding tough conversations. It means being present enough to notice what is happening and addressing it constructively. It is about fostering an environment where people feel safe, valued, and motivated to do their best work.

Think of emotions like water—they can Flow gently or carve through the rock over time. Leaders who adapt like water do not just manage challenges; they use them as moments to connect, grow, and transform.

Can you recall when emotions influenced a situation in your leadership experience? How did you respond, and what might you do differently to handle it with greater insight and intention next time?

REFLECTION 5.14

BREAKING THE CEILING – THE GROWTH MINDSET IMPERATIVE

"Life is not about finding yourself. Life is about creating yourself."
– George Bernard Shaw.

"Intelligence is fixed." "Leaders who succeed are naturally gifted." "Talent is something you either have or don't." How often have these limiting beliefs crept into our thinking? These are not just misconceptions—they are barriers that hold us back from realising our true potential as leaders. Yet, as researchers like Carol Dweck and Robert Sternberg remind us, Growth is not predetermined—it is a choice.

I recall working with an executive who seemed destined for great things. Yet his progress stopped—not because of a lack of talent but because of his reluctance to adapt. He clung to strategies that had worked in the past and was sure they would carry him forward. His fixed mindset became his ceiling, preventing him from seeing possibilities beyond his grasp.

In contrast, I remember another leader who faced a daunting failure—a project that had drained resources and morale. Instead of retreating into blame or defensiveness, she asked a simple but profound question: "What can we learn from this?" That moment of humility and curiosity transformed her leadership and revitalised her team. She understood that setbacks are not walls; they are doors waiting to be opened.

These experiences remind me that, as leaders, our mindset is a lens through which we view the world. It shapes our growth and the environment we create for those around us. When we embrace a growth mindset:

- Challenges become development opportunities.

- Feedback is no longer a critique but a gift for improvement.

- Failures lose their finality, becoming stepping stones instead of dead ends.

This is not to say growth is easy or always visible. Like the roots of a tree deepening unseen during harsh winters, actual growth often happens in quiet, unglamorous moments of reflection and perseverance. Growth does not mean endless progress; it means the belief that even during the most challenging times, something within us is expanding, preparing us for what is next.

Leaders who embrace growth inspire the same in their teams. By nurturing this mindset, you lay the foundation for resilience, innovation, and collective success.

Think about a moment when you felt stuck or limited by your assumptions. What held you back? How might adopting a growth mindset have opened a door to new possibilities? What can you do today to nurture a continuous growth mindset for yourself and those you lead?

REFLECTION 5.15

SHAPING TOMORROW – THE RESPONSIBILITY OF LEADERSHIP

"A solitary fantasy can transform a million realities."
– Maya Angelou.

Have you ever paused to envision the future—not just for yourself, but for the people you lead? Visionary leadership is like painting on a vast, blank canvas. Each idea, decision, and action is a stroke shaping the picture of tomorrow. But here is the challenge: Are you painting with intention and purpose, or are you letting uncertainty and distractions dictate the outcome?

I recall a conversation with a leader who felt frustrated by a disengaged team that seemed adrift. Though they had ambitious goals, they struggled to articulate them in a way that resonated. As a result, the team was unsure of where it was headed. That moment reinforced a critical truth: a vision is not just about having big dreams—it is about creating a picture so vivid that others can see it, believe in it, and work together to achieve it.

Visionary leadership is not about holding onto an idea in isolation. It is about inspiring others to share the same horizon. When leaders effectively communicate their vision, they spark energy, foster collaboration, and provide clarity even in the face of challenges. A clear vision shifts the focus from "What do we need to do?" to "What can we achieve together?"

Crafting a vision is just the beginning. A compelling vision must also be actionable. While dreaming boldly is essential, turning those dreams into a shared reality requires grounded steps and thoughtful guidance. Visionary leadership thrives at this intersection of imagination and execution.

Steps Toward Visionary Leadership

- Start with Purpose: Build a vision that aligns with your values and inspires those you lead.

- Engage Others: Involve your team to create shared ownership and align perspectives.

- Translate Vision into Action: Define concrete steps, set milestones, and sustain momentum.

- Adapt Without Losing Focus: When obstacles arise, refine your approach while staying true to the core vision.

Leadership is about creating paths where others see none—painting a future that inspires action and resilience. The strokes of your leadership—your decisions, clarity, and persistence—shape the journey for yourself and those who follow.

What vision do you hold for your team or organisation? How can you make it compelling, clear, and actionable? What steps will you take to turn that vision into a shared reality today?

CLOSING NOTE: LEADERSHIP: A RAINBOW OF INFLUENCE

"Leadership is the capacity to translate vision into reality."
– Warren Bennis, American Author on Leadership Studies.

Is there a single, universal definition of a leader? Certainly not. Like a rainbow, leadership is multifaceted—a spectrum of diverse hues, each representing unique styles, approaches, and impacts. While many may claim the title of leader, authentic leadership transcends self-proclamation. It is defined by the perceptions of those around us and shaped by a leader's character, choices, and courage to inspire meaningful change. Ultimately, leadership is about what one chooses to do with one's position and power. Like light passing through a prism, true leaders refract their power into a vibrant spectrum of influence, creating a legacy that lights the way for others.

Leadership is not merely about authority or status; it is an act of service and a commitment to transformative action. It demands the ability to envision possibilities and the will to bring them to life with care, authenticity, and intention.

The true measure of great leadership lies in the lives illuminated, the trust nurtured, and the futures shaped. As you reflect on your leadership journey, remember this: every decision you make, every relationship you build, and every vision you parade add a unique stroke of colour to your leadership spectrum. Lead boldly and authentically, and inspire others to join you in crafting a masterpiece of shared progress, purpose, and hope.

Part 6.0

SUCCESS: ENIGMATIC AVATARS

"Success is a journey inward, not a destination outward."
– Seneca.

Let us return to an age-old question: Am I successful? This rhetorical question often triggers a cascade of deeper inquiries. What is success? How do we define it? Success is not a fixed standard but a matter of perception. With nearly 8 billion people on this planet, there are 8 billion unique interpretations of success. Which one should we embrace? The answer is none. Success is deeply personal and shaped by our own experiences, values, and aspirations. It is not something others can define for us—it is a question only we can answer for ourselves.

This section explores success's many forms, each offering its own perspective and lessons. Success appears in different shapes throughout our lives, evolving with time and circumstances. While society often glorifies visible markers like promotions, wealth, and accolades, it can overshadow deeper truths—purpose, fulfilment, and alignment.

This chapter invites you to view success not as a final destination but as an ever-changing experience. It reflects the ongoing dialogue between our inner values and the external realities we face. Whether we celebrate, reflect on, or even redefine it, success is never static. It is a living paradox, urging us to question, grow, and embrace its many avatars and find the one that aligns with our inner self.

REFLECTION 6.1

VISION TO VELOCITY IS NO PROGRESS

*"Progress is not in enhancing what is, but advancing
toward what will be."*
- Khalil Gibran.

Progress is often celebrated as a hallmark of success. We are encouraged to push relentlessly, achieve milestones, and expand our horizons. Yet, the paradox of progress lies in its dual nature: while it can inspire growth, it can also leave us feeling unmoored, disconnected, and questioning the purpose of our journey. In chasing progress, we sometimes find that we have moved further away from the things that truly matter—our values, joy, and the meaning behind our efforts.

The true essence of progress lies not in velocity but in vision. Without purpose and alignment, speed becomes meaningless, and progress becomes an illusion.

I found this especially evident in the social sector. Many founders begin their journeys fuelled by passion and purpose, driven to create meaningful change. Over time, however, operational pressures, deadlines, and external expectations take over. The focus shifts from vision to velocity, impact on metrics, and the initial purpose starts fading. The result? Motion without meaning.

I have experienced this drift myself. There were moments when I was deeply engrossed in projects that appeared successful but left me questioning their true value. I realised that moving quickly—without direction—can leave us further from our goals, not closer to them. These experiences taught me an essential lesson: true progress is not about how fast we move but about where we are headed. It is about keeping vision as our guiding star.

To redefine progress, we must challenge the idea that speed equals success. Progress is not just motion; it is intentional and purposeful movement. Sometimes, it requires slowing down, recalibrating, or pausing to ensure our actions align with our values and long-term vision.

Velocity without vision is not progress; it is simply movement. True progress lies in balancing ambition with purpose, striving with clarity, and movement with mindfulness. It invites us to pause, reflect, and ask: Am I moving closer to what matters?

Progress is not a destination. It is a process of shaping our reality to reflect what truly matters.

How might you ensure your progress is guided by vision rather than driven by velocity? What changes could help you realign with your purpose and make your journey more meaningful?

REFLECTION 6.2

PROBLEMS AND SOLUTIONS: YIN AND YANG

"Every problem contains the seeds of its own solution."
– Norman Vincent Peale, American Minister and Author of
"The Power of Positive Thinking"

Have you ever felt like a big problem completely overshadowed everything else? It is easy to get stuck there—focusing so intently on the problem that the solution, sitting right on the other side, goes unnoticed. But here is the truth: Problems and solutions are not separate. They are like Yin and Yang, two forces that coexist, balancing and complementing each other. You cannot have one without the other.

Think about your own life for a moment. How often do we label something a "problem" and stop there without asking what it is trying to teach us? Problems feel heavy and complicated, but maybe they are not the enemy. Perhaps they are part of the story that helps us grow, adapt, and find clarity. We are writing this story—we play both the Protagonist and the Deuteragonist in our lives. We are not just the hero striving to overcome challenges; we are also the guide, the inner voice that helps the hero find their way forward.

No one else can play these roles for us. Waiting for someone to rescue us is like waiting for rain during a drought—it might happen, but it is faster and more reliable to start digging your own well. Being your own Deuteragonist is not glamorous. Solutions rarely arrive in perfect packages. They are messy and imperfect, but they move us forward. And that is what matters.

What if we stopped seeing problems as obstacles and started seeing them as opportunities? Opportunities to step up as both the hero and the guide in our own story. When we embrace this dual role, we take ownership of our challenges. We stop waiting for life to fix itself and start shaping it ourselves. As Winston Churchill said, "We are the masters of our destiny." Is not that empowering?

Solutions do not come from an external source swooping in to save the day. They come from within us—our ability to pause, reflect, and take intentional action. Progress is not about perfection; it is about momentum. It is about realising that problems and solutions are two sides of the same coin, each pushing us closer to balance and harmony.

How can you step into both roles—the hero and the guide—in your current challenge? What small action could help you take ownership of the solution already waiting within?

Reflection 6.3

THE TRUTH ABOUT LUCK: READINESS

"Luck is what happens when preparation meets opportunity."
– Seneca.

Timing often feels like the ultimate game-changer. We have all seen someone land a big break or achieve something extraordinary simply because they were in the right place at the right time. But here is the paradox: timing might open a door, but our readiness determines whether we can proceed.

Timing can feel frustratingly random. A perfect opportunity might present itself when personal responsibilities or a lack of resources make acting impossible. In those moments, it is tempting to blame lousy timing or luck. But readiness—not timing—defines our capacity to seize opportunities. Readiness is not just about having the right skills; it is about mental clarity, emotional resilience, and the ability to act decisively when the moment arrives.

Leadership offers countless examples of this principle in action. Consider Winston Churchill during World War II. His career had seen significant ups and downs, and by the late 1930s, many regarded him as politically irrelevant. Yet, he spent years studying military strategy, honing his rhetoric, and building resilience. When the moment arrived in 1940, with Britain urgently needing strong leadership, Churchill was ready. His preparation allowed him to rise to the occasion and lead his nation through one of its darkest hours.

Similarly, consider Abraham Lincoln. Lincoln faced numerous failures before becoming the 16th president, from lost elections to personal struggles. Yet, he used those experiences to develop empathy, perseverance, and a deep understanding of human nature. When the Civil War erupted, Lincoln's readiness to navigate complexity and unite a divided nation made him one of history's most iconic leaders.

Looking back, there were times in my life when I felt left behind, as though I was not in the right place at the right time. Over time, I realised that the opportunities I thought I missed were not failures. They were the moments when I was not ready. Timing is rarely within our control, but staying prepared means that when the right opportunity does come, we are ready to meet it.

Readiness is more than preparation; it is a state of being. It is about aligning your mindset, honing your skills, and cultivating resilience. The timing paradox teaches us that we cannot control when the moment will come, but we can control how prepared we are to embrace it. As Churchill and Lincoln exemplified, readiness involves continuous growth and preparation, even when the future seems uncertain. Their stories remind us that luck favours the prepared.

Luck, after all, is not something we find—it is something we create through readiness.

What does readiness mean, and how can you prepare for future opportunities?

REFLECTION 6.4

SUCCESS WITHOUT INTEGRITY IS FAILURE

"Success will come and go, but integrity is forever."
– Amy Rees Anderson, American Investor and Philanthropist.

What is success if it rests on shaky ground? It is not just about having a bold vision or relentless drive—it is about integrity and purpose. This foundation ensures that your creation is meaningful, sustainable, and trustworthy.

I once met a healthcare founder with a groundbreaking idea. The potential impact was enormous, and the buzz around their venture was palpable. But when initial testing fell short, they made a tough call: to pause and reevaluate before moving forward. It was not an easy decision, and they risked losing momentum and funding. But that pause reinforced their credibility. It was not about rushing to market but delivering something that truly mattered.

Consider the stark contrast between the healthcare founder's approach and that of Theranos, a company that became a cautionary tale in the business world. While the founder's decision to pause and reevaluate reinforced their credibility, Theranos' ambitious claims lacked sufficient validation, leading to its failure to deliver its promises. The fallout affected stakeholders and employees, underscoring the critical importance of rigorous validation and transparency in building trust. The Theranos story serves as a stark reminder of the role of integrity in ensuring that ambition aligns with accountability.

Integrity of purpose requires courage. It asks tough questions:

- Are we solving the problem we set out to solve?
- Have we tested this enough to stand behind it?
- Are we willing to walk away if it does not serve its purpose?

Asking these questions is not a sign of weakness—it is a display of strength. Integrity ensures that success is not just a momentary win but something that leaves a lasting impact. Without it, even the brightest ideas can crumble under their own weight.

How do you ensure your choices reflect integrity when faced with a difficult decision? How can you ensure integrity remains at the heart of your options and actions?

REFLECTION 6.5

SUCCESS DEMANDS INTENSIVE PURSUIT

*"Success is no accident. It is hard work, perseverance, learning,
studying, sacrifice, and most of all, love for your actions."*
– Pelé (Edson Arantes do Nascimento), Brazilian Football Legend.

As Pelé asserts, success demands relentless effort. But is it just about working harder? The answer lies in the intensity of pursuit—a focused, unwavering drive to achieve your goals.

Consider Infosys, one of India's most iconic IT companies. In its earliest days, the founders worked out of a cramped apartment, pooling their limited resources and relying on sheer determination to break into the global market. Their passion was undeniable, but their measured, intentional, and collaborative intensity set them apart. They did not just work harder; they worked smarter—adapting and aligning their efforts with their long-term vision.

Similarly, Serena Williams, widely regarded as one of the greatest tennis players of all time, embodies this principle. Her success was not merely the result of raw talent but a product of disciplined, focused intensity. Serena practised relentlessly, studied her opponents, and refined her skills over decades. Yet, her pursuit was not confined to the court—it extended to her mindset. Despite injuries, personal challenges, and defeats, she maintained her clarity of purpose, demonstrating how sustained intensity can fuel excellence.

But here is the catch: intensity without direction can lead to burnout. I have seen founders and teams relentlessly chase progress, only to lose sight of what truly matters—health, relationships, and the purpose behind their efforts. Passion alone is not enough; it needs clarity, focus, and alignment to sustain the journey.

Intensity is not limited to individual leaders or star performers. For any venture to thrive, the entire team must share that drive. When everyone embodies the same spirit, even chaos feels purposeful.

Intensity is not about sacrificing balance; it is about aligning every action with the goal, knowing when to push and when to pause. It is not about how hard you work—it is about working with heart, clarity, and intention.

What does intensity mean to you, and how can you sustain it without losing focus or balance?

REFLECTION 6.6

SIZE AND AGE: NO GUARANTORS OF SUCCESS

"It is not the strongest of the species that survive, nor the most intelligent, but the one most responsive to change."
– Charles Darwin.

For decades, success has often been equated with size and longevity. Large corporations with a long history were seen as invincible, with their resources, reputation, and reach giving them an apparent edge. But history has repeatedly shown that neither size nor age is a safeguard against failure.

Take Nokia—once a global leader synonymous with innovation, it felt invincible at its peak. However, when the smartphone revolution arrived, Nokia failed to adapt. Its size and deep pockets could not save it from losing relevance in a rapidly evolving market. Nokia's story is a stark reminder that success is not inherent to being big or established—it is about staying agile, humble, and relevant.

Consider General Motors (GM), a company with over a century of history. Once the world's largest car manufacturer, GM faced bankruptcy in 2009 due to its inability to adapt to changing consumer preferences and economic realities. While GM ultimately restructured and recovered, the crisis highlighted that even decades of dominance can crumble when complacency and short-term thinking prevail.

The Success Traps:

1. **Arrogance Creeps In**: Leaders assume what worked yesterday will work forever.
2. **Complacency Takes Hold:** Organisations cling to the familiar, resisting the need for change.
3. **Short-Term Thinking Prevails:** Chasing quarterly results blinds leadership to long-term sustainability.

Large, long-established corporations that thrive are those willing to question themselves. They adapt, innovate, and embrace humility. I once worked with a company on the brink of irrelevance. Instead of clinging to their legacy, they embraced change, letting their employees and customers guide their reinvention. It was not easy, but it was transformative.

Success is not about size, age, or resources but agility and purpose. Without them, even the mightiest corporations risk fading into obscurity. Success is not the *Swadharama* of large corporates.

How can your organisation break free from the success traps? How can leadership balance humility, agility, and purpose?

REFLECTION 6.7

SUFFOCATED SOUL: LOSING THE WAY TO SUCCESS

"Culture eats strategy for breakfast."
– Peter Drucker.

Every organisation has two sides: the tangible and the intangible. The tangible side—the systems, processes, and infrastructure—is easy to see and measure. This gross body, the visible machinery, keeps things running. But then there's the subtle body—the invisible essence of values, culture, and ethos. It is harder to measure but truly defines an organisation's soul.

Think of it like a ship. The gross body is the hull, sturdy and essential, while the subtle body is the compass guiding the way. Without both, the boat is lost. Yet, the subtle body often goes unnoticed—until it falters.

Here is the paradox: success, while celebrated, can weaken the subtle body. Success brings recognition and resources but can also bring arrogance, complacency, and bureaucracy. I have seen organisations so focused on their achievements that they lose sight of their core. Trust erodes, innovation slows, and purpose fades.

One company I worked with prided itself on a strong culture. Creativity and collaboration were its lifeblood. But as success grew, so did its hierarchy. Meetings became about approvals, not ideas. The open-door policies they once championed disappeared, and employee engagement plummeted. Success had subtly shifted their values.

The subtle body is fragile because it thrives on alignment and shared purpose. These are not things you can write into a policy—they are nurtured through actions, leadership behaviour, and staying true to your ethos.

Nurturing the subtle body is not about rigid rules but integrity in action. It is about aligning what you do with what you value. It is about evolving without losing yourself—adapting to change while holding onto what makes you unique.

The subtle body is the heart of an organisation. Nurture it, and it will guide you through the storms. Neglect it, and even the most substantial organisation can drift off course.

How does your organisation's culture reflect its values? What steps can you take to nurture trust, alignment, and purpose?

REFLECTION 6.8

SUCCESS IS FRAGILE: HANDLE WITH CARE

"It is not the load that breaks you down, it's the way you carry it."
– Lou Holtz, American Football Coach.

At its peak, success feels unassailable. Yet, the pandemic showed how fragile it truly is. What seemed like steadfast achievements—thriving businesses, expanding economies, carefully planned lives—collapsed under the weight of an invisible force. COVID-19 did not just shake the foundations; it shattered illusions of permanence.

Looking back, it is clear that success was never as secure as we believed. Enterprises that scaled aggressively, fuelled by debt and an insatiable hunger for growth, were the first to falter in the "whirlpool" of collapsing demand. Individuals who measured success by external milestones found their carefully constructed lives upended overnight. Like patients with preexisting conditions, businesses and lives burdened by hidden flaws proved the most vulnerable to disruption.

Yet, disruption carries its lessons. Does success's fleeting nature diminish its value? Or does it reveal that true success is not about avoiding disruption but thriving through it? The pandemic highlighted the paradox of success: It rewards consistency but demands adaptability when the ground shifts beneath us.

The Buddhist principle of impermanence (*Anityavada*)— the idea that all things are transient—offers a lens through which to view this moment. Nothing is permanent—not our struggles or triumphs. Disrupted certainty forces us to rethink success, not as an endpoint but as a process—a journey of reimagining purpose, recalibrating priorities, and building resilience.

Success, after all, is fragile. Handle it with care—by staying adaptable, grounded, and purpose-driven.

How has the disruption of certainty during COVID reshaped your understanding of what it means to be successful?

REFLECTION 6.9

DISRUPT SUCCESS TO REALIGN

"Adversity is like a strong wind. It tears away from us all but the things that cannot be torn so that we see ourselves as we really are."
– Arthur Golden, Memoirs of a Geisha.

What did COVID do to us? It disrupted our successes and achievements, forcing many of us back to a zero-sum game. An invisible force levelled businesses, economies, and carefully crafted personal milestones, leaving us scrambling to find footing in a transformed world. Success, which once felt secure, suddenly felt fragile, and control seemed to slip through our fingers.

The pandemic did not just destabilise; it demanded a complete rethinking of what success and control truly mean. Businesses driven by aggressive scaling, fuelled by debt and relentless growth, suddenly hit a wall. High debt and low margins placed many in the "Red Zone," where survival became challenging. In contrast, companies prioritising resilience—low debt, diversified supply chains, and adaptability—were better equipped to weather the storm.

For individuals, too, COVID upended ambitions and forced us to confront uncomfortable truths. What did we truly need versus what we wanted? Retreats were no longer defeats but recalibration. Many of us let go of outdated success metrics and learned to focus on what truly mattered—health, relationships, and purpose.

Here is the paradox: sometimes success must be disrupted for us to realign with what truly matters. Disruption is not about failure; it is about breaking free from patterns that no longer serve us. The pandemic offered a harsh but necessary reminder: control is not about avoiding chaos but navigating it with clarity and purpose. Disruption clears the clutter, revealing what truly matters. It dismantles barriers, guiding us to realign our actions with our values.

As Sun Tzu wisely said, "In the midst of chaos, there is also opportunity." Disruption provides the chance to reassess, strengthen, and adapt. It forces us to ask hard questions: What matters most? What do we need to leave behind to move forward? Many found opportunities within adversity—new careers, innovative ideas, or unexpected personal growth. It is in these moments of recalibration that true resilience is born.

Looking back, I see that COVID's disruption was not just a setback—it was an opportunity to regain control by reshaping our priorities. Success is not a linear path but a dynamic process of realignment and reinvention. To move forward, we must be willing to disrupt comfort for clarity and embrace the challenges that lead us closer to purpose.

What parts of your life or work were disrupted by COVID, and how have you adapted? How can intentional disruption help you regain control over your path to success? How can you use disruption as a deliberate strategy to realign your goals with your values?

REFLECTION **6.10**

WHEN SUCCESS TEMPLATES FAIL

"In preparing for battle, I have always found that plans are useless,
but planning is indispensable."
– Dwight D. Eisenhower (34th President of the United States
(1953–1961).

Crude oil prices have long been a cornerstone of global economic success. Conventional wisdom dictated that when oil prices drop, oil-importing nations benefit—lower energy costs, reduced inflation, and economic growth. The success template seemed simple and reliable: cheaper oil fuel recovery.

But COVID-19 unexpectedly upended this predictable formula. The dramatic drop in crude prices, which should have been a blessing for buyer countries, became irrelevant in the face of demand destruction. Widespread lockdowns halted industries, and reduced consumer spending wiped out the expected benefits of low oil prices.

Take India as an example. Initially, the government saw an opportunity in plummeting crude prices and began stockpiling oil in anticipation of an economic boost. Yet, the anticipated gains evaporated as demand collapsed globally. Industries like aviation, automotive, and tourism, which should have thrived with cheaper energy, were crippled by shifting consumer behaviour and uncertainty. Instead of driving growth, the drop in oil prices became a missed opportunity.

The paradox is stark: The pandemic's disruption nullified a universally accepted template for success—lower crude prices driving economic recovery. However, the template did not guarantee success; it was contingent on a stable ecosystem that no longer existed.

This is not just an economic lesson; it is a broader reminder about the fragility of success templates. Established formulas work only under predictable conditions; even the most reliable pathways to success can collapse when disruptions strike.

COVID forced us to rethink our economies and personal measures of success. The domino effect of lower oil prices, which should have sparked growth, serves as a warning: success is not about clinging to rigid templates but embracing adaptability and resilience in the face of disruption.

As Eisenhower aptly said, "Plans are useless, but planning is indispensable." Success in a disrupted world requires preparation, adaptability, and the willingness to rethink assumptions. To thrive, we must embrace uncertainty, question established norms, and develop strategies to pivot when the unexpected happens.

How can you develop strategies to stay adaptable and resilient when established success templates fail?

REFLECTION 6.11

THE COURAGE TO NOT KNOW

"Real knowledge is to know the extent of one's ignorance."
– Confucius.

Admitting "I do not know" is one of leadership's hardest yet most transformative acts. Acknowledging uncertainty can feel like a weakness in a world that prizes certainty, metrics, and best practices. Yet, this very humility often leads to deeper and more meaningful success.

As historian Yuval Noah Harari observed, "Twenty-first-century humans are far more ignorant than we realise." Despite access to endless data, algorithms, and case studies, these tools often create an illusion of certainty rather than broadening our understanding. Instead of opening new doors, they reinforce what we believe, closing our eyes to alternative perspectives and untapped opportunities.

This paradox is particularly evident in leadership. I have seen boardrooms filled with leaders celebrated for their achievements, equating success with complete understanding. They speak with unshakeable certainty, often dismissing differing viewpoints. And yet, the most transformative leaders I've encountered are those who dare to say, "I don't know." These leaders understand that real success emerges not from certainty but curiosity—not from having all the answers but from asking the right questions.

This tendency becomes sharper with success. Past achievements often become blinders, convincing us that what worked before will work again. I have witnessed organisations falter because they clung too tightly to their formulas for success, unable to adapt to shifting circumstances. In contrast, those who embraced humility and maintained a learner's mindset often reinvented themselves, achieving success not once but repeatedly.

The wisdom of success lies not in accumulating knowledge but in the courage to question it. As Confucius reminds us, "Real knowledge is to know the extent of one's ignorance." Success is not about knowing everything—it is about remaining open to understanding. In embracing uncertainty, we create space for growth, reinvention, and deeper connections to what truly matters.

When was the last time your certainty about success was challenged? How might embracing "not knowing" lead to new opportunities and achievements?

REFLECTION 6.12

PEACE THROUGH CONFLICT – A MIRAGE?

"Peace cannot be kept by force; it can only be achieved by understanding."
– Albert Einstein.

Can war truly lead to peace, or is it an illusion we have perpetuated throughout history? The notion of success through conflict has shaped human civilisations for centuries. Today, with two significant wars and nearly 30 conflicts raging globally, the paradox of war as a path to peace feels more glaring than ever. What we consider advancement often reflects a deeper contradiction: Are we truly progressing or simply repeating history in different forms?

War promises peace but delivers paradox. Research reveals a decline in the Global Peace Index across 111 countries, with political and religious disputes driving significant fatalities. Strikingly, neither secular ideologies nor theocratic systems have consistently fostered peace. Even nations celebrated for democracy and progress often fail to transcend cycles of conflict. These patterns highlight a disquieting truth: the traditional definition of success—achieved through dominance or victory—rarely translates into lasting peace or progress.

This paradox applies not just to nations but also to individuals and organisations. Like nations at war, we often pursue victories—career milestones, financial goals, or personal triumphs—believing they will bring peace or fulfilment. Yet, what happens when these victories feel hollow?

The pandemic amplified this question for many of us, forcing a reevaluation of what truly matters.

The way forward lies in redefining success. True success is not about conquering or dominating—it is about fostering harmony within ourselves and others. Two pillars support this vision: freedom and faith.

- **Freedom goes beyond political liberty:** it is about liberating ourselves from political, ideological, or personal dogmas. True freedom creates space for dialogue, understanding, and coexistence.

- **Faith transcends rigid institutions:** It is about faith in humanity—compassion, empathy, and a shared sense of purpose. This faith nurtures connection over conflict and understanding over division.

This vision may seem idealistic, but isn't it worth striving for? These same principles apply to personal success. True fulfilment comes not from relentless striving or domination but from aligning our values with our actions and cultivating meaningful connections.

As Einstein wisely reminds us, "Peace cannot be kept by force; it can only be achieved by understanding." Success demands the courage to move beyond the illusion of victory and embrace the profound work of creating harmony on both global and personal levels.

How has the pursuit of personal victories mirrored the illusion of success through conflict? If we prioritise harmony over triumph, how might that reshape our understanding of success?

CLOSING NOTE:
DEFINE YOUR AVATAR

"Success is not the key to happiness. Happiness is the key to success. If you love what you are doing, you will be successful."
– Albert Schweitzer—Theologian, Philosopher, Physician and Nobel Peace Prize winner (1952).

After reflecting on the 12 themes of success explored in this part, an inevitable question arises: Is success absolute, relative, deceptive, or merely a fleeting and alluring emotion? Or is it an act of self-proclamation? As we have discovered, success is multifaceted and demanding, shaped by time and context yet elusive in its essence. It remains one of the most heavily interpreted—and misinterpreted—pursuits, endlessly chased for its often dangerously attractive allure.

Having grasped its intriguing and intricate nature, should we remain indifferent to success or continue to chase it? Whatever path we choose, one thing is clear: we must first define what success truly means to us. Without that clarity, we risk climbing a ladder leaning against the wrong wall, only to regret the journey at its end. Intentionality, grounded in self-awareness, is the foundation of any meaningful effort in life.

It is equally important to acknowledge that success is born from a complex interplay of factors. While our efforts play a significant role, they do not guarantee results. Even the hardest work and the most intense dedication may fail to deliver the anticipated outcomes. Moreover, our perceptions of effort are often skewed—misbalanced or misjudged—adding to the enigma of success.

Another common pitfall is assigning universality to success. Society often imposes universal markers—wealth, status, accolades—but we are under no obligation to conform to these constructs. Success is not a one-size-fits-all journey; it is deeply personal, shaped by our unique values, aspirations, and circumstances. By rejecting society's imposed definitions, we liberate ourselves to pursue success on our own terms, aligning it with what truly resonates within us.

Ultimately, success should reflect who we truly are, not a shadow of others' expectations. By embracing this truth, we gain the freedom to craft a path uniquely our own—one that brings both achievement and fulfilment. After all, the journey matters as much as the destination.

THE FINAL REFLECTION

The Promised Compass

"By three methods we may learn wisdom: first, by reflection, which is the noblest; second, by imitation, which is the easiest; and third, by experience, which is the bitterest."
– Confucius.

Ancient wisdom has long upheld reflection as the highest path to wisdom. Meaningful action follows a natural hierarchy: Observation → Reflection → Action. When reflection does not precede action, decisions often become misguided or incomplete.

Throughout this book, we have explored more than 90 reflections designed to inform and challenge. They invite you to question assumptions, explore unseen possibilities, and uncover pathways that may have gone unnoticed.

At their core, these reflections are more than ideas; they are a compass—guiding you through your journey's paradoxes, challenges, and triumphs.

You may have resonated with themes of self-discovery, societal paradoxes, or the workplace jungles, navigating the questions of success, self-worth, and purpose. Perhaps you've confronted the overwhelming expectations and enigmatic avatars of success that society presents.

As I mentioned in the Foreword, the Greek philosopher Heraclitus reminds us:

"Nothing exists except atoms and space; everything else is opinion."

This profound truth suggests that life is ever-changing, and much of what we perceive is shaped by opinions rather than absolutes. Should an opinion dictate how we live? Surely not. Yet, when approached with clarity, opinions can open pathways that align with our deepest values, lighting the way toward a more meaningful existence.

Returning to the Ignored Mirror

What does the Ignored Mirror reflect on you? Does it reveal your true self, your inner agency? Look deeply, and let it question you. But be cautious—mirrors can deceive, just as in Oscar Wilde's tale of Dorian Gray, where the pursuit of external perfection led to inner corruption.

Your roles, accolades, and milestones are simply means to an end, not the end itself. The Ultimate End is constant and quietly persistent, yet it is often ignored as we chase fleeting illusions of success.

This mirror calls upon you to pause, reflect, and realign—to embrace the truths that anchor your inner self.

Reflection is not about self-judgement. Throughout history, the concepts of right and wrong, truth and illusion have been relative. What holds absolute truth is what brings you inner joy.

This joy belongs to you alone, not as part of a collective definition of success. Discovering this truth requires introspection, authenticity, and clarity—unclouded by others' opinions or societal expectations. This journey demands courage, resilience, and an unwavering commitment to self-discovery.

Making the Insights Work: The Promised Compass

The compass that guides your transformative journey whispers constantly. It offers four key directions:

1. **Pause and Reflect**—Develop the habit of asking, "Are my values aligned? Are my actions purposeful?"
2. **Lead Authentically** – True leadership is not about authority but service and integrity. "To lead by example is the most powerful way to lead." – Confucius
3. **Embrace Flux** – Every challenge is a stepping stone. As Nietzsche said, "What does not kill me makes me stronger."
4. **Act with Intention** – Every choice, no matter how small, shapes your journey. As Lao Tzu reminds us, "The journey of a thousand miles begins with a single step."

Over to You

Your journey begins with a question: **Did I discover the compass or create it—one reflection at a time?**

The answer lies in how you choose to step forward. Will you continue to examine your life, confront its paradoxes, and dare to live authentically?

Society will test you, for it is not only kaleidoscopic but occasionally uncanny. The corporate or workplace jungle will challenge your resolve and demand resilience. Yet, the mirror will not ask for perfection—it will ask for reflection.

It will ask: **Did you dare to reflect? Did you dare to live?**

Here is a paradox: The more we strive to perfect our external world, the more disconnected we become from our inner truth. Yet, the closer we align with our values, the more harmonious our external world becomes.

The Stoic philosopher Marcus Aurelius complements this thought: **"The soul becomes dyed with the colour of its thoughts. Guard accordingly and entertain no notions unsuitable to virtue and reason."**

Living by Your Compass

Success, peace, and fulfilment are not external prizes—they are reflections of who we are becoming through our choices, courage, and authenticity. Stand firm in life's paradoxes. They are not barriers but signposts. Embrace them as teachers, not adversaries.

Let your values and authenticity guide you like the North Star—constant and unwavering amidst life's changes. Every choice you make shapes your life and the lives you touch. Your reflections shape your intentions, and your actions bring them to life.

Transcend with grace and courage. Dare to reflect deeply, live intentionally, and step boldly.

A life true to your inner compass—aligned with your values—is well-examined and truly well-lived.

The Ultimate Realisation: The Promised Land Lies Within

The Promised Compass does not lead to a distant destination. It leads to the fulfilment that already lies within us.

It is not about chasing more—it is about being more.

As the Katha Upanishad (2.2.13) wisely says:

"When a person knows the self as pure and unchanging, as the witness of all experiences, and aligns with the eternal truth within, they transcend all sorrow and attain peace."

May your reflections light the way to Peace.

9 798897 245697